Last Things

Social work with the dying and bereaved

Edited by Terry Philpot

GW00690944

COMMUNITY
CARE
THE INDEPENDENT VOICE OF SOCIAL WORK

1989

Last Things
Social work with the dying and bereaved

Published in 1989 by
Reed Business Publishing/*Community Care*
Carew House, Station Approach, Wallington,
Surrey SM6 0DX

Set in 11/11 Souvenir Light and Printed in Great Britain
by Geo. H. Hine & Co., Limited,
Bury St. Edmunds, Suffolk

Contents

Contributors

DIANA DAVENPORT
Qualified nursery nurse and a foster mother for almost 30 years. Author of *Adoption and the Coloured Child* and *One Parent Families: A Practical Guide to Coping*.

GILLIAN FORD
Deputy chief medical officer, DHSS on secondment to St Christopher's Hospice, London, where she is director of studies. Author of "Terminal care in the National Health Service" in *The Management of Terminal Malignant Disease* (edited by C Saunders).

MOTHER FRANCES DOMINICA
Qualified nurse and founder and director of Helen House, Oxford. Author of numerous papers including "The nursing care of the chronically sick or handicapped child" in *The Physically Handicapped Child* (edited by G T McCarthy).

JULIA FRANKLIN
Social worker, Bloomsbury Support Team, London. Secretary, Association of Hospice Social Workers.

CHRIS HANVEY
Assistant director, National Children's Home. Author of *Social Work with Mentally Handicapped People*.

JUDY HILDEBRAND
Freelance trainer, therapist and conciliator and former senior social worker, Hospital for Sick Children, Great Ormond Street, London. Clinical consultant with the Institute of Family Therapy. Author of numerous papers including a chapter on group work in *Child Sexual abuse within the Family* (edited by A Bentovim et al.).

MICHAEL HOLLINGS
Catholic priest at St Mary of the Angels, London and dean of North Kensington. Author of *Living Priesthood*, *Prayers before and after Bereavement*, *Alive to Death* and *You are not Alone*.

BEL MOONEY
Journalist and novelist.

MAUREEN OSWIN
Author of *Behavioural Problems amongst Children Living in Long-Stay Hospitals*, *Holes in the Welfare Net*, and *They Keep Going Away*.

TERRY PHILPOT
Editor, *Community Care* and editor-in-chief, *Social Services Insight.*

PETER PRITCHARD
General practitioner in Oxfordshire. Former part-time tutor Barnett House and Ruskin College, University of Oxford. Author of *Manual of Primary Health Care* and *Management in General Practice* and various publications on patient participation and general practice topics.

SYLVIA POSS
National training manager, Family and Marriage Society, South Africa. Former medical social worker and head of the department of social work, Johannesburg Hospital. Author of *Towards Death with Dignity.*

LESLEY REILLY
Social worker, Staincliffe General Hospital, Dewsbury. Social work practice teacher who is also involved in midwifery training.

ELIZABETH EARNSHAW-SMITH
Senior social worker, St Christopher's Hospice, London.

ALISON WERTHEIMER
Freelance writer and researcher, currently researching a book on the experiences of people bereaved by suicide. Former director of the Campaign for People with Mental Handicap and policy officer, MIND.

Introduction

Terry Philpot

The much greater professional interest shown in dying and bereavement in recent years, and the attendant burgeoning literature, has been at variance with public attitudes which have pushed death more and more from the general gaze. In his seminal work, *Death, Grief and Mourning in Contemporary Britain* (Cressett Press 1965) Geoffrey Gorer remarked upon "a shift in prudery" so that sex had become more directly and naturally spoken of, while natural death (as opposed to violent death in books, horror comics, film, and television) had become evermore unmentionable.

There are many reasons for this. Life, in the Western countries at least, is no longer nasty, brutish and short, its content can be fuller, its span longer, and the expectation now is of long life rather than early death. For the most part, too, death, like birth, does not take place in the family home, bodies are no longer laid out in a coffin in the parlour where neighbours, friends and relatives can pay their final respects. It has become professionalised: its habitation is the hospital and before burial, the body rests in the undertaker's chapel, where far fewer people, either by inclination or for practical reasons, choose to view it. Perhaps, too, a more secular age dwells more on what this life has to offer than the prospects of what might come hereafter.

Whatever the reasons, too often the result of this hiding away of death has been, as Carole Smith writes (*Social Work with the Dying and Bereaved*. Macmillan. 1982), "anxiety, confusion, uncertainty and embarrassment". Undoubtedly, the growth of the hospice movement has done much to create a greater understanding of how both dying and bereaved people need to be cared for. The hospice has not only pioneered the judicious use of drugs in pain relief, it has shown the qualities which the professional helper needs.

Yet social workers cannot work in this field without facing their own anxieties, fears and fact of their mortality; they, too, then, need to be clear in their own minds about their attitudes toward the subject, their philosophies of life (and death).

As doctors may have a particular problem facing death because it may seem to them to be a denial of their efforts, to offer no hope of cure or the restoration of health, to challenge their whole professional *raison d'etre*; so, too, social workers: death is not subject to change, it cannot be ameliorated or modified. The traditional social work aims may seem, at first sight, useless in the face of such remorseless finality. In such circumstances, what the social worker might elsewhere attempt to achieve needs not so much to be reversed as to be set aside. Thus, she must come to realise that in helping the dying and bereaved activity and optimism are not required but rather it is pain and sorrow, even despair which have to be worked with and that they will be overcome only by death itself. But this is not to suggest that such work dwells on the negative; the opposite is true, for from the experience of working with dying people and those who will mourn their loss may come a real understanding of faith, courage, fortitude, quiet acceptance, even growth. Love, pleasure, companionship, a sense of worth and dignity will be as evident in facing death as they can be in the rest of life. It is the social worker's task – as it is that of other professionals – to help the dying person live as fully as possible until he dies.

Social work does not come to loss as a latecomer behind other professions like nursing and medicine. Helping coping with loss is very much a part of the social worker's job: the child who is being adopted and faces new, unfamiliar and even frightening surroundings; the elderly person entering residential care; people facing rehousing away from a physical and social environment which they have enjoyed for years; the partners in divorce – all of these, and others, are part and parcel of the everyday challenge to good social work practice.

This book, then, is published in the belief that the social worker has an essential place in the care of dying people and those who are bereaved and that, for example, offering practical assistance and listening, two very different but important tasks which are particularly the social worker's, are elements without which such care would be seriously deficient.

There is now a great library on death and bereavement, an unfortunately small part of which only has been written specifically with the social worker in mind. That, too, is the intention of this book but it also offers a multi-disciplinary perspective. While it is hoped that it will prove useful to other types of professional, it is aimed at imparting knowledge and skills most directly appropriate to the social worker and to show how a multi-disciplinary perspective bears upon social work practice in this area.

The chapters by professional contributors have been complemented by the last three chapters written by three women who have, in different ways, been bereaved – by the loss of a child through stillbirth, a father through illness, and a son through suicide.

In attempting to shut death out of life, in pushing it to the corners of our experience and (no doubt we hope) our psyche, we also succeed in forgetting that death is a condition of life. For all of us it is a dangerously self-deluding mistake to believe otherwise for unless we understand this, life itself is out of balance. Those who seek to help the dying and those who grieve must hold before them, as must all of us if we wish to be fully human, the words of Rabindranath Tagore's *The Stray Birds*:

Death belongs to life as birth does.

The walk is in the raising of the foot as in the laying of it down.

Terry Philpot
Surrey
January 1989

For convenience the dying or bereaved person is referred to in the text in the male gender and the carer or spouse (save in actual case studies) in the feminine.

1

An overview

Sylvia Poss

Among the wealth of available literature on the topic of death and dying it is difficult to extract a core that will set the scene for this book. Instead I shall try to do so by relying on my own work with dying people, their families, and their caregivers (Poss 1981). My aim is to offer some principles towards caring for the patient and his family, so that the crisis can be mastered with dignity. A review of the literature is not my purpose.

I write here of the caring work that is done directly with the patient and his family. That is not to say that social work in the terminal care field involves only direct clinical work (or casework). There is much scope for working with groups – of patients, relatives, team members, and/or professional and volunteer caregivers. Community work is widely needed in terminal care work to raise consciousness of the issues involved, develop services, and involve consumer and citizen participation in issues of death and dying that affect us all. There are also serious implications in terminal care work for social work supervision, education, and management, which all merit discussion, and should be borne in mind, as a backdrop to this book.

I shall, however, confine myself here to a brief discussion of some principles of direct care.

The most helpful perspective I know from which to view terminal care and bereavement work is that of perceiving death as a natural event in the process of life and living. In this context, life consists of many stages each with a beginning and an ending, and each leading on to a new beginning – as does death. I write with the conviction that the dying person begins life in the hereafter and his survivors begin life in another role, as survivors: widow, orphan, bereaved, etc.

Since death is a natural life event, it is possible, as in the mastery of other life crises, for the individual to use his dying as an opportunity to develop and grow emotionally and spiritually in this life stage. Thus growth in the dying person lies in working both towards a dignified death and in preparing for life after death. As in any other life crisis, considerable work is involved in this adjustment, work which each patient must do for himself, and which significant others or caregivers in his environment can facilitate or hinder.

Whether the patient grows in stature or not during this final life crisis will depend in part on how he has managed other life situations. In this sense, the way he approaches death is likely to be a reflection of his adjustment in life.

Growth is more likely if some preparation is possible. Preparation is essential for any difficult life event, not least so for approaching death. Crisis theory reminds us that all of life constitutes "preparation" for our current life stage and the next one. Thus the way the patient has lived may be viewed as preparation for his dying but, in addition, he may benefit from specific preparation, conscious and unconscious, for this complicated event, if he knows of its approach. Hence the patient and his relatives who are confronted by sudden and unexpected death will not have had the same opportunities to prepare themselves, as those who have been ill over some time.

At the same time, while the patient is struggling to master his crisis, his relatives are involved in a life crisis of their own, that of coming to terms with the loss of a loved one. Their adjustment also involves work (hence "grief work"), which can either be facilitated or hindered, depending on the circumstances.

Happily, many families make these adjustments without needing professional or social work help. They may draw on supports within their immediate or extended family, neighbourhood, community, church, employing organisation, and/or health services. It is often the family who does not have these supports, or who is in some kind of difficulty, prior to the onset of the terminal situation, that is likely to need social work help with the terminal crisis.

Many disciplines need to be involved in terminal care. No one profession holds the monopoly for such care. Hence, whatever social work service is rendered, it is always offered in relation to the rest of a caring team. But the need for a "primary caregiver" emerges, that is, one professional person who will, on behalf of the entire team, carry out the major part of the psycho-social and spiritual work involved in facilitating the patient's resolution of the terminal crisis. In addition, a primary *family* caregiver may well also emerge, "someone emotionally close to the patient, and the physician's closest ally", as Abrams (1974) puts it.

Principles of terminal caring

From amongst the explosion of work in the field of terminal care and bereavement over the past two decades, several principles of care have emerged. I shall list here those that have proved most useful to me in my work. These are principles for caregiving in general rather than specifically for social workers. Obviously, they need to be super-imposed onto social work's body of knowledge and skills.

COMMUNICATION

Communication with the patient is central to all care. Unfortunately, the word has become clichéd through overuse. Often we pay only lip service to the concept and continue to talk *about* the dying or bereaved person, instead of *with* him. We "tell" or "advise", with the very best intentions, instead of listening to what *his* need and focus are. We decide for him, "on his behalf", since "he is in no fit state to decide for himself", instead of assisting him to make his own decisions right to the end. We keep the truth from him, thinking that "He can't take it" and "We had best protect him", instead of recognising that that protection is for ourselves, and that we are insulting him and putting him down. We certainly treat him differently from how we would wish to be treated ourselves under such circumstances, while claiming (smugly) to be "loving our neighbour as ourselves".

Real communication remains thus the first principle of care to attend to. It involves listening carefully and persistently, to verbal and non-verbal messages, to what is said, and what is felt behind the words, and to what remains unsaid because it is too difficult to put into words. It involves the basic social work principles of "Begin where the client is" and "Move at the patient's pace" (Garrat 1970) where possible, allowing him self-determination, listening with non-judgemental acceptance, and being able to stay there, even when it becomes uncomfortable to do so, for example, during a silence, while the listener is feeling helpless and inadequate, and when the patient, eventually, comes face to face with the realisation that he is dying.

Paradoxically, communication does *not* involve much talking, and certainly does *not* require that answers be given to the patient's questions – and especially not to questions like "Am I dying?" or "Will I get better?" Instead, a reflective statement, or another question, for example "*You* feel you are . . .?", or "What makes you think so?", or "I guess you must be wondering about that . . ." will further the patient's *work* of coming to terms with what is happening to him and let the listener off the hook!

In considering communication with the patient, the controversial question inevitably arises: "Should the doctor tell?" Because it is such a vexed and crucial issue, I shall offer my thoughts on the matter. I suggest that the patient – centered principle again provides a guide. Thus: should one tell? If the patient asks, asks persistently, and poses a real question, rather than asking for reassurance – e.g. "What is wrong with me?" rather than "I am not going to die, am I?" – then I estimate that any caregiver would have a clear indication that this patient *wants* to know, and could be guided by that fact.

16

Why should one tell? I feel strongly on this point that honesty gives the patient the opportunity to use his foreshortened time profitably to prepare for his oncoming death appropriately, so that he may, for example, live his life to the full, while he can. Honesty in this sense may not necessitate giving answers, but may mean staying with the patient and reflecting his questions, so that he can continue to stay in touch with his own oncoming death and continue to *work* with its implications.

What should one tell? I suggest that the caregiver could answer one question at a time, and as much as the patient asks for. I make a distinction here between answering some questions factually, as opposed to communicating with the patient in a non-directive way which allows him to continue to work on his awareness until he answers his own questions for himself. Both have a place in terminal care. Thus "What is wrong with me?" depending on to whom the question is put, may be answered with "You have a tumour that needs to be removed", or with "What do you think is wrong?", or "What guesses have you made so far?"

Depending on what the patient's response is, the need to give further information (or not) will emerge. Another question, like "Why must the tumour be removed?" will require further fact, whereas, "I think I have cancer . . ." may require a silent staying with the patient while he digests that fact. In contrast, "I don't know what is wrong with me – You tell me" may require confrontation ("You're wanting me to put into words what seems difficult for you to think about?") or empathy ("It's hard not to know what is going on . . .") or support ("I'll stay with you, while you think it all through once more . . .").

When should one tell? I believe that the right time to tell is when the patient asks! This may be a moment of great inconvenience to the caregiver, but indicates the patient's readiness to hear.

How should one tell? I suggest short, simple, honest words, preferably using the patient's own phrases or language, and not complicated medical terms. The principles of sound communication – enumerated above – may serve as a guide.

Who should be the one to tell? Ideally, I believe the person to whom the question is put – the one the *patient* trusts enough to ask, is in a good position to answer. This notion implies teamwork, in which each member of the team would know enough to answer honestly and be skilled enough to answer the patient's questions, in a facilitative way, although I know that this is not always possible.

Thus, communication involves honesty, even if that involves discomfort. It does not involve game-playing with the patient, his relatives, or his survivors.

17

JUDGEMENT

A second principle of (terminal) caring states: judge each case on its own merit. It is impossible to prescribe care. Each situation is unique and demands the benefit of objective assessment, rather than a recipe – like guide, or "one form of treatment for all" which is often the one preferred stance of the doctor-in-charge, developed to help him avoid what is emotionally uncomfortable for him.

Objective assessment of each case may be aided by using Kübler-Ross's (1970) now classic guide of sequential emotional stages of progress towards acceptance of death. The stages through which the patient passes are – as most readers will by now know – denial, isolation, anger, bargaining, depression, and then acceptance.

Another means of assessment may lie in considering some of the tasks involved in coming to terms with the crisis of approaching death (Poss 1981). Hence one could ask: with which of these six tasks does this patient appear to be preoccupied at present?

- ☐ Becoming aware of impending death.
- ☐ Balancing hope and fear throughout the crisis.
- ☐ Taking an active decision to reverse physical survival processes in order to die.
- ☐ Relinquishing responsibility and independence.
- ☐ Separating the self from former experiences.
- ☐ Preparing the soul for death.

The patient's pattern of coping in the past will also serve as a useful way of assessing his capacity to cope with this present crisis. Especially significant will be how he had adjusted to other situations involving loss. Hence, the patient who has lived his whole life with denial is unlikely, now, to want to know the full truth of his current circumstances.

ATTENTION TO DETAIL

Dame Cecily Saunders, founder and first medical director of St Christopher's Hospice, London, suggests a third principle of terminal and bereavement caregiving: pay attention to detail. Hence, although the patient may be dying of abdominal obstruction, if *his* complaint is of constipation or a toe nail that needs cutting, those details must be attended to, in order for him to feel respected, cared for, and safe. Such requests may be made to divert the patient's own attention away from the too-frightening reality of his dying, or to reassure himself that he *is* being listened to, or to maintain his self-esteem by looking decent, and so on. Whatever the probably complicated reason, these simple tasks should be responded to as efficiently and purposefully as the rest of his care.

PAIN CONTROL

Saunders enumerates a further principle of care: control the pain. This injunction refers to *any* pain – physical, social, emotional, and/or spiritual. Happily, major progress in medical science has yielded an array of analgesics, which, given regularly and with sufficient strength, will hold the pain at bay, while allowing the patient enough clarity to function mentally, without inducing addiction. Emotional, social, and spiritual pain bring us back again to the subject of communication, as it is only when we *listen* that we will hear what the patient's pain is, and so be able to give him the opportunity of working through it.

HELP THE PATIENT TO LIVE

Another principle of terminal and bereavement care is: help the person to *live* until he dies. This statement implies distinguishing quality from quantity of life. It may mean asking "unspeakable" questions like "Given that you have less rather than more time left, what do you want to do with it?" or "If you *were* out of hospital and well, what would you want to do?" Such questions are likely to lead to some consideration of life's unfinished business – a will to write, a hobby to indulge in, a creative outlet that demands fulfilment, or a relationship to "put right". I suggest that the patient be helped to do whatever it is he so badly wants to do, however unlikely it may sound, so that he can then let it go and journey on.

With bereavement, the corollary task to helping the patient to live until he dies is likely to relate to the loved one who has recently died, with whom something feels unfinished or disturbing. The completion work can be encouraged in thought, prayer, role play, the "empty chair" situation and the like, so that the departed one can be left behind, and the surviving person too can journey on.

MOURNING

The care of the bereaved person requires a special word. Mourning needs to be regarded as a natural, healthy, healing process which should not be suppressed by drugs. Since loss of a loved one is regarded as among the highest stress factors in life (Arbose 1979), the more the survivors are helped, before and after the death, to feel their pain and to express it, the less likelihood there will be of psychiatric ill-effects later in life. Those who stand by may well feel helpless to ease the distress. They should be encouraged not to move away, but to stay there, so that the healing process can proceed without added complications.

SPIRITUAL CARE

It is essential to consider what spiritual care each patient may need, and to make it available to him, in response to his own unique need. Once the dying person becomes aware of his impending death, he is likely to ponder on what lies beyond life or some aspect of that which lies beyond death may somehow be presented to him by way of preparation. In this vein many patients have reported their experiences of glimpsing another world (Osis 1961), seeing or meeting with a loved one already dead, or, in rare instances, with a biblical character (Moody 1976), and (Hinton 1968) has reported that many patients have been observed to turn, return, or draw closer to God in preparation for death. Consequently, concern and discussion about religious issues are appropriate during this stage of adjustment (Carlozzi 1968). In some cases, in fact, acceptance of death is synonymous with calm faith or peace (Kübler-Ross 1970). In this sense, the dignity of dying refers to the dignity of an arisen soul.

A key issue with which the dying person contends is thus a spiritual one. The soul's preparation for death appears to require as much work, involve as much of a struggle, and demand as much realistic acknowledgement of the pain of dying as death's emotional adjustment demands. Spiritual preparation may therefore be described as the ultimate terminal problem-solving task. Religion does not obviate the conflicts of the crisis; it should, however, provide the various participants in the situation with the strength to face and resolve them. An explanation of the importance of this terminal task may be that the soul, or ego, senses that it is about to be liberated. Thus energy formerly used for physical survival is now diverted towards enhanced spiritual development. In this sense the decision to reverse survival processes involves man's free will; the giving over and relinquishing tasks constitute acts of trusting or submitting to the will of God; and the disengagement involves not only the detachment of self from life, but the separation of the soul from the body. There is, thus, a constant interweaving of emotional and spiritual work. For the unbelieving patient this task may take the form of evaluating his life experiences in order to reach an integrated whole.

Caring for the caregivers

As important as caring for the patient is another principle of care that is receiving more and more attention: care of the carers.

Caring for dying and bereaved people and their families takes its toll on the caregivers. It is not easy to be in constant, close contact with suffering, helplessness, uncertainty, pain, and death. While this work is continuously experienced as complicated, those very encounters with difficulty, uncertainty, and pain, which yield no apparent results, may be useful to the caregiver in keeping her in touch with some of what her patient is enduring. On the other hand, once work with a dying patient seems easy, the caregiver is likely to be colluding, denying, or blocking some of the patient's experience. Consequently, it may be worth considering what resources and supports are available to help caregivers in their difficult task.

TRAINING

What do we need, in the way of training, to equip ourselves as caregivers? The skills required for terminal and bereavement caring are those required in any other field of social work, care or counselling, perhaps augmented by one additional skill – the ability to tolerate close contact with dying and death. Professional credentials and fields of specialisation are less important than the capacity to be there, to have the ability to contain, or "hold", the emotions which the patient experiences, which enable him, eventually, to bear these feelings himself. This stance involves resisting the strong temptation to avoid any confrontation of the real issues at stake, and, instead dealing with them, as honestly, directly, immediately, and simply as possible. Such honest containment rules out "kindness". The task of the caregiver is to facilitate the conscious experience of what is happening to the patient, based on the conviction that a constructive and supported experience of conflict or difficulty can be creative.

HOPE

Elements of hope and therapeutic enthusiasm are vital forces in any helping situation. Both the patient, his relatives, and the caregivers need to maintain hope, in order to continue their work, and reach acceptance. In the terminal situation, hope implies realistic optimism, and not denial, collusion, or unrealistic work aiming only for a "cure".

SOME WAY OF MAKING SENSE OF THIS DIFFICULT SITUATION

The faith of the caregiver – if she has such – also constitutes a vital element in the situation, in that it is likely to carry the conviction that there can be meaning in suffering and in dying;

that it is possible for man to accept impending death; that a supernatural force is present, loving, and caring and giving strength enough to bear all that is permitted; and that life after death is a reality (which implies that the struggle involved in dying with dignity may be viewed as a preparation for life in another dimension). Player (1954) reminds us that: "Even if for the social worker herself any organized religion may appear unnecessary, it is only realistic to know that for her client, it may be the most important thing in life." If, therefore, the caregiver feels unable to respond appropriately to the patient's spiritual preparation for death, she should draw the minister of religion into the caregiving team.

STRESS MANAGEMENT AND PREVENTING BURNOUT

Terminal caregiving requires sound organisational structures and policies, as well as mature management (Moos 1984). Colleagues, supervisors, or managers, need to understand their role in providing support, opportunities for ventilation, challenge and teaching. Regular appraisal of how one is doing is a vital element in coming to terms with the work, or with the fact that one is not suited to it, and needs to leave.

The rewards for such work are considerable. Not only does one have the satisfaction of knowing that one has cared for a fellow human being at his most vulnerable, but, at the same time, our experience and familiarity with death and dying equips each one of us to face our own death with greater preparation and acceptance. There is something awesome and precious about accompanying a person who is about to face his creator. That awe and privilege accompany *us*, as we journey on to our next life task.

Poss, S *Towards Death with Dignity*. George Allen & Unwin. 1981.

Abrams, R D *Not Alone with Cancer*. Charles C. Thomas. Springfield, Illinois. 1974.

Garrat, A *Interviewing: Its Principles and Methods*. Family Service Association of America. New York. 1970.

Kübler-Ross, E *On Death and Dying*. Tavistock. 1970.

Poss, S. *Op. cit.* Chapter 2, "Adjustment to the prospect of death".

Arbose, Jules (ed), "Home truths about stress" in *International Management*. Feb. 1979, pp. 42, 43.

Osis, K. *Deathbed Observations by Physicians and Nurses*. Parapsychology Foundation. New York. 1961.

Moody, R A *Life After Death*. Bantam Books. New York. 1976.

Hinton, J *Dying*. Penguin. 1968.

Carlozzi, C G *Death and Contemporary Man: The Crisis of Terminal Illness*. William E Eerdmans. Grand Rapids, Michigan. 1968.

Kübler-Ross, E *On Death and Dying*. Tavistock. 1970.

Player, A "Casework in Terminal Illness", *The Almoner*. Vol. 6, No. 11, Feb. 1954, pp. 447–88.

Moos, R H "The Crisis of Treatment: Stress on Staff" in *Coping with Physical Illness 11: New Perspectives*. Plenum. New York. 1984.

2

Working with bereaved families
Judy Hildebrand

This chapter argues in favour of a shift away from working with bereaved individuals and, where possible, towards adopting a family focus. Everyone involved in a family or social network is affected by a bereavement, whatever the nature of the loss. In my view, only offering individual help to the bereaved may preclude, or at least inhibit, much of the therapeutic value to be gained by people sharing their feelings with their own family and friends at a time of crisis.

Traditionally however, the vast majority of professionals and volunteers in this field worked on an individual basis with their client or patient, and many still feel most comfortable operating in this way. On the other hand there are encouraging signs that many workers are learning and applying ideas and skills derived from groupwork and from family therapy. Whilst appreciating the value of an individual approach, their horizons are broadening, and they are taking a fresh perspective and focussing on bereavement in a wider social and family context. They realise that working with a family can provide opportunities for each person to share their feelings, to learn how others feel, to clarify the details of the loss and gradually to consider how they can all contribute to coping with the inevitable changes that follow a bereavement. Surely the value of this approach must lie in grieving together, in helping and being helped. After all, loss is a normal and inevitable part of life; such experiences are not "pathological" and only rarely require treatment. Seeing a person individually can sometimes imply that there is something "wrong" with that person. We all know that while there are no cures and solutions to loss, nevertheless we can help people to share their pain, their anger and even their relief with each other. In other words, we can help them to mourn. For many people nowadays, the religious and cultural rituals of mourning no longer seem relevant or acceptable; therefore it is all the more important that we offer the bereaved an opportunity to take part in a process which is both personal and social.

In the current political climate, inadequate resources are allocated to bereavement work and we therefore need to maximise the help that is available. In my view, seeing the whole family together on one or just a few occasions can be as effective and further reaching than protracted work with an individual. The aim of the family approach is to build on the existing strengths within each family and to encourage them to help each other through the mourning process, rather than to become dependent on a voluntary or professional worker whose contact is of necessity limited. In this way, people who normally would not ask for help or be referred can also be included in the healing process.

Clearly, there will be many cases in which it is not possible to meet with the whole family but, even so, this should not stop us from taking a wider perspective. It can be argued that when working with an individual you can nonetheless "include" many of his relevant family and social circle as if they were present. For example: "If you and your wife had not separated, how do you think you would have coped with your daughter's hospitalisation? If she were here now what do you think she might suggest?"

This could open up fruitful discussion of the earlier "loss" of his wife when they separated as well as his current fears about his daughter dying in hospital. It might also help him to consider alternative ways of managing and perhaps also whether to include his wife in the meetings.

Like the man in the example, many people become quite overwhelmed by their loss, wrapped in an isolating cocoon of misery. They are unable to recognise how others may also be suffering. As workers, we can help to bring people together in order to discuss their mutual worries and to negotiate how they will cope in the future.

The following example illustrates how we can help people to share their situations with others in their own social network. "Your mother sounds like a lovely lady, I imagine that many people will miss her. Do you think there was anyone close to your mother who would appreciate having a chance to talk to you about her?" This approach helps the client to realise that others will also miss his mother, that grief is normal, that there may be an opportunity for him to share his grief, not with a stranger but with someone who also cared for her.

Sometimes a worker's own view of how a client should mourn prevents her from understanding the communications made by the client. For example, a counsellor was worried that she was making no headway with a client because the client refused to discuss her bereavement any more. However, I also learnt from the counsellor that in fact several changes had already taken place which she hadn't perceived as particularly significant. The client had stopped wearing black, was attending a social group for the bereaved and was knitting a jumper for a grandchild! Clearly she was communicating her improved state, albeit not verbally.

In another case example, a social worker was concerned about a couple's reaction to an accident in which their 21-year-old son John was killed, and the father escaped without injury.

The father refused to discuss the death and the social worker felt she had been unable to help. What she did not recognise was the strength, support and love that John's friends were giving to his parents. Although they rarely talked about the accident during their visits, the parents were helped to face their loss and to feel less isolated. That was their way of mourning at that stage.

PREPARATION

Taking a family approach is a challenge and many workers express anxieties about how they can possibly help everyone in the family. I see the task as helping all the individuals involved to recognise that their group has a shared loss, as well as the potential to support each other, and that it is not for the worker to provide solutions. As noted in the third and fourth examples above, the solutions considered appropriate by the workers were not relevant to the clients at that point.

There are some useful ways to prepare oneself for this work.

Personal considerations

If we work with the bereaved, surely we should be prepared to face not only our own experiences of loss but also how we did or did not cope with them. Equally we have to face our own mortality. If we are not in touch with these issues, we are more than likely to feel overwhelmed by the pain of others and to proffer "solutions". Apart from being compassionate and sensitive to each family's loss, we must also present a model that in time, however agonising, pain and loss can be contained as life goes on.

FAMILY PAST AND PRESENT

In preparing to work with the family it is helpful to discover how they functioned prior to the loss, and what they now see as their major problem.

A 42-year-old woman and her younger husband had had difficulty in conceiving and she then miscarried at two and a half months. The worker felt that their grief was out of all proportion until she realised that it was now very unlikely that the couple would have another child, given their fertility problems and her age. Not only were they grieving for this lost baby, but also for any others they might have had. They were also anxious about the effect of this loss on their relationship.

THINKING ABOUT CHILDREN

Some workers are worried about working with a family if they have not had much direct experience with children. Some find the open expression of children's sadness too painful.

The worker might find it helpful to prepare herself for understanding how children feel by doing the following exercise. Try to recall your earliest experience of loss: How old were you? Can you think of two or three words to describe how you felt then? What would have helped? Who could have helped? Would that be somebody known to you or a stranger?

Too often children are confused, misunderstand, feel to blame or guilty, feel no-one tells them what is going on or really comforts them; adults often pretend that everything in the family is fine when clearly it is not. Many of us are drawn into this work through personal experience, which may heighten our sensitivity to pain and distress, but, if we are not careful, we may also be tempted to console or protect children inappropriately. Our task is to help the child's family network do that.

As preparation for working with children in families, do consider their age and stage of development. For example, following the death of her husband, an angry, distraught woman said of her 16-year-old son Paul: "I don't understand him, he doesn't care, he hasn't shed a tear." I talked to the family about the different ways in which people grieve, and commented on the half/child, half/adult feelings adolescents experience. The mother slowly began to recognise her son's anguish and to realise that he was frightened of showing how he felt in case he made her feel worse. His father had always been stoical and Paul felt the manly thing to do was to keep a stiff upper lip. When his mother heard him say this, they were then able to cry together and eventually talked about how they might manage a future without dad.

In another case, a family came to see me worried about how they were coping with the death of their 21-year-old son in an industrial accident. Their daughter, Kathleen, aged 19, was able to grieve with her parents and talk about their bereavement. During our meeting, however, it became increasingly clear that she felt very guilty about continuing at college and was very worried about whether it was reasonable for her to still enjoy going out with her friends. As they described their tragic loss we all cried together and finally I said: "As an experienced counsellor, I can offer you nothing that you don't already know; you've all managed so well and unselfishly. If the Church offers you solace, that is fine and appropriate. As for Kathleen, like you I know the important thing for young people is to retain their energy, to feel alive and to have permission to move on. I recognise your deep love for Kathleen and for each other and as a parent I know that your loss can never be made good, but I also see that you can give each other comfort and that you both want Kathleen to continue living."

I did not offer them a further meeting and this was intentional as I wanted to emphasise the view I had expressed, namely that they were coping as well as any family could in the circumstances.

Communication

If, as I assume, we feel that it is helpful for the bereaved to express their feelings, this process can be encouraged by using words and concepts that are clear and unambiguous. In this way it is more likely that everyone present can make sense of what is being said. In addition, we may have to initiate communication about painful "hidden" issues, which the family may avoid, but which may inhibit their mourning process if not dealt with.

A general practitioner referred a family to a child psychiatric department following a fatal accident in which the mother died. The doctor's concern was about the younger child Stefan, a boy of eight; no mention was made of Gloria, his 11-year-old sister. However, he did disclose that prior to the accident, Stefan had been referred for a psychological assessment because of poor school achievement; the parents had been referred for marriage guidance because of difficulties in their relationship and the father had been attending a psychotherapist to try and deal with his persistent drinking problem.

It was clear that relationships in this family had been complex indeed. My aim was to focus on the family as a unit, to try and help them share their grief and to be clear about both the death and how they might cope together in the future. I asked them to describe what they knew of their mother's accident and discovered that Gloria felt she had been careless and therefore contributed to her mother's death. Her father then explained what had happened which clearly demonstrated that neither child could have had any responsibility for the death. We then went on to talk about how things were different at home now and what changes there would be in their everyday life, without their mother. Given the family's previous difficulties I then went on to tackle what I thought might be their underlying concerns: "Some children I've talked to have been quite worried about whether their father could manage things on his own; perhaps you even worry that your dad might start drinking too much again and then what would happen to you."

In this way, I took responsibility for communicating about hidden worries. If I had commented on an issue which was not particularly relevant to that family, that would soon become clear from their verbal and non-verbal responses. If that was the case I would acknowledge that in my effort to "guess" what they might be feeling, I had got it wrong and really needed their help to understand what was troubling them.

By talking in terms of "some children", I was trying to communicate the idea that some other children had also had terrible losses. The intention here is not in any way to minimise their tragedy, but to demonstrate that those other children did survive, and that on top of their current misery they did not need to feel so different or isolated from their peers. This technique is perhaps most helpful to avoid putting pressure on children to respond; I saw no reason to address questions directly on this issue nor to exact answers. Children can communicate their feelings very well; observe their sudden stillness as they listen – or the apparently unrelated comment or interruption – or how they sometimes turn to the surviving parent to silently ask permission to talk about their loss. In this case, Gloria responded by being very critical of her father until he explained who would be looking after them when he was at work; she said she had been worried that there wouldn't be anyone to help her choose clothes and talk to her. He explained the new domestic arrangements to the children and reassured them that if things started to go wrong he would tell them. I felt that Gloria had also been worried about whether she would have to be grown-up and look after her brother – and possibly her father – or whether she could still be a little girl. I made a comment to this effect but did not pursue the issue; I knew it had been heard.

I feel that clear and open communication in families is far more likely to be achieved when everyone is seen together. Had I seen the members of this family individually, they would not have had this firsthand experience of being with someone who encouraged and helped them to share their feelings and to exchange information immediately. To see the children separately might have made them feel "put on the spot", "at fault", or "odd". In addition, their father already had an individual therapist to support him. Seeing the family together on three occasions seemed both more relevant and economic.

After all, our task is to help people to acknowledge and come to terms with their loss. Our involvement is inevitably and appropriately time-limited, while the potential for family members to help each other is life-long. Thus, seeing the family together discourages further fragmentation, provides a model for open communication in the future and prevents the worker from acting inappropriately as a temporary go-between.

The bereaved are sometimes described by well-intentioned and frustrated workers as uncommunicative, unresponsive, unwilling to talk, stuck or resistant. I do sometimes wonder how much we miss of the many different ways in which people communicate their feelings. Although unrecognised by the worker previously mentioned, the client clearly demonstrated her emergence from deep mourning not in discussion but in her behaviour, that is by no longer wearing black. Children often have much to say via their play and their drawings, but all too often the worker does not pay sufficient attention to their offerings. The following example demonstrates my own slowness in recognising a child's communication.

An interesting feature of the family work with Stefan and Gloria was that Stefan refused to speak at all for two interviews! However although he refused to talk, he drew non-stop. When I belatedly suggested drawing a family tree as a way of uniting his form of communication and mine, he grasped the opportunity and talked freely while drawing. He then asked me how he should show that his mother was dead. It seemed too insensitive to suggest putting a line through her or making a cross as people usually do when drawing a family tree, so instead I asked them all what they thought. Stefan immediately said "I know" and drew a rectangular grave with roses growing around it. This case confirmed the importance of recognising and using the natural ways in which children communicate.

Working with the terminally ill

In families with a terminally ill member, there is often a great deal of controversy about whether or not to communicate openly with the patient and his family about the seriousness of the situation. Currently the decision is generally taken by a medical practitioner, presumably on the grounds of knowledge of the patient's physical condition. In my view, however, this is an ethical, and not a medical, consideration. The dying person, primarily, and then his family and friends must have the option of dealing with the situation as they wish. Ultimately we must take our cue from the individual and his family and not impose our own beliefs. Clearly, our own practice reflects our personal or agency view, and I think that, intentionally or otherwise, we all tend to convey our own beliefs in these situations. Perhaps the best we can do is help families face the possible implications of both sharing knowledge and maintaining a silence, remembering that in many instances there are religious or culturally prescribed responses to loss which we should also respect.

My own clinical experience suggests that where anticipatory mourning is possible and where family and friends do have an opportunity to share their feelings with the dying person, it is less traumatic for them subsequently. There has at least been an opportunity to talk, to share feelings and to make arrangements.

Mrs L was slowly dying and was under constant treatment. Her two teenage daughters were given a variety of reasons for the hospital visits but were never told of the probability of their mother dying. Mrs L refused to allow the severity of her illness to be discussed; "being strong", as she put it, was the only way she could force herself to carry on. I therefore only met the parents. I respected her point of view but felt it necessary to mention some of the ways in which the whole family might be affected by her decision. I said I wondered if the family would be given an opportunity to help her or enough time to say goodbye. I wondered if they hadn't already sensed the serious nature of her illness and whether it might be a relief to know exactly what was happening so that they could share the load. I also asked if she felt it might help her husband to know that he could talk openly to his daughters. I admired her courage and determination but just gently suggested that in time she might allow herself some comfort from those who loved her most. Had the children been present with their mother's permission, I might have asked: "I wonder how anyone would know if your mother needed some help, how can you tell when she's down?"

In this case, although I felt it would have been an enormous emotional relief for the situation to be made clear I also respected Mrs L's wishes to remain in control for as long as possible. Interestingly, the following example demonstrates the opposite way in which another family dealt with terminal illness!

The W family had known all about Mrs W's fatal illness for two years. They talked openly together as a family about how life was before she became ill and how their mother had organised the house to make it easier for their father to manage; and how they gradually had to adapt to "her having breakfast in bed every day" and then going into hospital to die. In this case one family meeting was sufficient to confirm that Mr W was coping very well with his 13, 10 and five-year-old children. In our meeting Mr W was able to say that since his wife's death he had learnt that it was alright to ask for help and he realised that he had friends to whom he could turn for practical and personal support. His eldest son was finally able to say that he really couldn't always manage to be stoical. His sister managed to be angry and expressed her confusion about being the only female left in the family and whether she should now take charge.

This family, seen only four weeks after Mrs W's death and at the request of a hospital consultant, was able to describe the mother, talk about the illness, express their sadness and anger, laugh warmly and appropriately together with the five year old, and ask questions. Their tragedy is enormous but because of the parents' preparation, openness and concern for them, I think they are unlikely to feel as guilty or confused or to blame as many families do following a bereavement.

Depending on our own beliefs and experience we may feel that we know what is "best" for a dying person; but do we? One person may wish to be surrounded by family or friends, another simply to be contained.

In *A Reckoning*, May Sarton (1978) most movingly describes the death of an older woman. What becomes increasingly clear is the character's need to choose her own manner of dying, of finding out who and what has been significant in her life. She feels burdened by the good intentions of her caring family and solicitous doctor. Eventually even her faithful dog's paw becomes too heavy on her lap, and although she truly treasures the picture her artist son paints for her as a last loving gift, she finds it too vibrant to look at. The proximity of her caring family is sometimes too much to bear. The solace and simple physical comfort and containment of a stranger who nurses her at the end provides greater security: the nurse has no expectations of her patient.

To have been able to provide a family meeting with her adult children and grand-children might have supported them in sharing the very different ways they had felt about their mother and their loss; and it might have helped them to understand her need to divest herself of their loving concern.

In this chapter I am advocating a shift towards working with bereaved families rather than focussing on individuals, and have suggested that, in the words of Gelcer (1983), "mourning is a family affair". A family is far greater than the sum of its membership and the challenge for us is to work with the family group, focussing on its characteristics and interactions rather than on each member in turn. Clearly, there will be many situations in which it will not be possible to see all the family, but this should not preclude us from using a wider perspective where possible. The majority of people do not live in isolation and we may need to encourage them to recognise any potential strength and support to be found in their own families and networks. In some cases seeing individuals can lead to an inappropriate dependency on the worker and in such instances the "loss" of the worker may be experienced as yet another bereavement.

Bereavement is a particularly painful area for clients and workers alike; whether working in a professional or a voluntary capacity, it is essential for those who undertake this work to have some training in this field. As the bereaved individual needs support from his family and social network, so we as workers must ensure that sensitive and experienced regular support is available to us also. Of necessity our work involves helping clients to mourn and to adapt constructively to severe loss which often means quite a radical change in their lifestyle and attitude. Can we as professional or voluntary workers make an equally radical change in our approach to clients?

Black, D "Mourning and the family developments" in *Family Therapy*. Ed Waldron-Skinner, S. Routledge & Kegan Paul. 1981.
Gelcer, E "Mourning is a family affair". *Family Processes*. December, Vol. 22, No. 4 December 1983.

Hildebrand, J "Counselling bereaved families". *Bereavement Care* Vol. 4, No. 2. Summer 1985.

Hildebrand, J "Engagement and joining: Preparatory processes to counselling and family work". *Journal of British Association for Counselling.* February 1985.

Lonsdale, G, Elfer, P & Ballard, R "Children, grief and social work". *The Practice of Social Work* No. 4. Blackwell. 1984.

Raphael, B *The Anatomy of Bereavement* Hutchinson. 1984.

Sarton, M *A Reckoning* Women's Press. 1978.

I would like to thank Helen Curtis for her generous help in preparing this chapter and Anne Krish, who constructively commented both on the issues and the text.

3

Terminal care teams

Julia Franklin

Malignant disease is an emotive topic, cancer an emotive word. Sometimes positive gains are made from the publicity around cancer in terms of finance raised for research, etc. but the negative side of the coin is that the general public often see pain, suffering and death always being the out-come following the diagnosis of cancer. On the other hand, the hospice movement in recent years has shown the needs of patients and their families can be met. This has been a contributory factor to support teams being established all over the country.

Terminal care support team, home care team, Macmillan team, pain and symptom control team are some of the titles given to teams of professionals dealing with patients who are terminally ill and their families, either in hospital, in the community or moving between the two. There are also hospices and continuing care units, some with home care teams attached, but for the purposes of this chapter, I am using the experience from, and concentrating on, teams with no specific links with hospices but whose patients are suffering from terminal cancer or specific symptoms caused by malignant disease. I have drawn on information from social workers attached to teams in the London area.

There is a valid argument that patients and their families suffering from chronic disablement and diseases for which there is no cure could use the facilities and resources offered to cancer patients and their families, that is the multidisciplinary team approach to the problem of long-term sickness with its ripple effect on family and community resources. The focus of involvement of this sort of team, and the time span necessary to be planned for, would be different from the terminal care support team dealing with cancer patients; however, there are similar needs in these patients and their families for support and the chance to work through losses as they arise.

The setting up of terminal care support teams is a relatively new idea, a new specialism, and in London most of the social workers have been appointed in newly created posts. Some of the social workers work part time, some full time. One team has been established several years, others are only in the process of being set up. One team was axed in a round of cut-backs in 1984; some teams have links with particular hospitals and service large areas; some are funded by the NHS, others by voluntary resources; and at least one of the social worker's posts is joint-funded. This mixture of experience in just one area – London – in 1984 is a reflection of what is happening in other parts of the country at the present time.

There are many factors at work when the setting up of a terminal care support team is being considered. Among the altruistic ideals for patients and family to receive better care and pain and symptom control may not be such altruistic ideals (but nevertheless important considerations) such as the saving of money, and the movement of patients more quickly from acute hospitals beds home again.

There is no doubt that thorough planning based on re-searched local needs, by the people in authority in the various disciplines required, is the best start to the setting up of a team. Sometimes a community pressure group will have been active in drawing attention to the needs of an area but much of the success of such teams being set up is related to the groundwork having its roots in the commitment of such people as the community health council, social services department, district medical teams and community nursing officers to the idea of linking hospital and community care for the benefit of patient and family.

A key issue may well be whether the different disciplines at this high level are able to work and plan together. Sometimes teams do not get off the ground, or take a considerable time in so doing because of this very problem.

Sometimes, however, the timing being right for whatever reason, is the particular boost necessary to the setting up of such a team. For example, the present emphasis on community care, is focussing attention on services being provided in and by the community, to enable people to stay in their homes as long as possible. This may well be a key factor in getting a scheme introduced in a particular area, particularly if the emphasis of such teams is to be advisory and educative, with its function being to work alongside resources already in the community, such as general practitioners, community nursing services and social service departments.

Careful planning before the appointment of staff is very important, giving particular thought to the number of and level of personnel to be appointed, the siting of office accommoda-tion and making provision for the funding of office furniture and the administrative back-up necessary for such a team. Planning and funding a multidisciplinary team often requires much flexi-bility and trust between planning team members as money for salaries and equipment for the various personnel will come from NHS, area health authority, community and social services, all of whom have particular and consistent constraints on their resources and differing priorities for its allocation. Allocating money to the care of the dying may be a priority which has not been rated high in past traditions of provision in the NHS or social services. Sometimes terminal care support teams are initially funded by the Macmillan Fund or other charities, with a view to the local health authority and social services taking over the costs at a later date.

The appointment of team members is another very important issue. Sometimes individuals appointed to form a team find they can work together by a happy accident; by chance their ideas about patient care and the role of the team coincide and they are able to form a cohesive unit which will help them get through many of the teething troubles which beset terminal care support teams in their infancy. Unhappily, this is not always the case.

A new team needs the mutual support of its members in working out what its ethos will be; how to cope when morale is low; when the work of the team is undermined, undervalued or misunderstood; sharing the pain and frustrations of working with difficult patients and their families; sharing the sadness and pressure of continually working with dying and bereavement. A team which is cohesive and mutually supportive can discuss these problems and grow in attempting to resolve them together. A team split by professional wrangling and personality clashes will find it more difficult to work cohesively and patient care may well suffer as a result. Supervision and back-up for team members is an important issue. Social workers have supervision built into their work structure, but this is often a new concept for nurses and doctors to understand and value.

The aims and purposes of a terminal care support team are threefold. It is an advisory and educative service on 24 hour call to assist the existing caring services in the hospital and community in providing optimal relief of any unpleasant or distressing aspects of terminal illness whether physical, social, psychological or spiritual. It provides a link for patients and their families between hospital and community. Lastly, it offers bereavement counselling and, if necessary, continuing support to those carers previously identified as being at risk.

How each individual team defines its role and carries out its aims and purposes will depend on its structure and how many people there are within the team. Important considerations are the essentially advisory and educative nature of the service and the multidisciplinary aspects of the intervention.

It makes sense to bring together in a team members of the medical, nursing and social work professions (sometimes with the added help of a hospital chaplain as the patients' problems are seen as not only medical but probably requiring nursing, practical, emotional spiritual and psychological help in the process of adjusting to the terminal phase of an illness). The link between the patients' pain, for example, and their increasing realisation and knowledge about the terminal nature of their disease, highlights the need for the various professions to be able to share their skills in finding the most appropriate way to relieve the pain. Full assessment of patients and family is often a very crucial element in the management of the symptoms.

St Thomas's home care team has been established for some years. It is based at St Thomas' Hospital in London and covers a large catchment area south of the river. This team has often been used as a model for other teams with modifications to adapt it to local needs. Some teams use a medical model as a structure for their organisation, that is, there is a consultant in charge, registrars, clinical assistants, nurses and social worker with the added resource of physiotherapists and occupational therapists. However, this is not the norm in the time of financial constraint.

Most teams have to function on a limited budget and may consequently have to choose more flexible models on which to base their practice using the physiotherapists and occupational resources which are already based in the community. Much will depend on the personalities of the people within the team whether there is a formal or informal structure to the way they work. There is a large amount of flexibility in practice which can allow for experimentation in multidisciplinary ways of working. As times goes by other models are emerging which appear to enable a team to achieve cohesion and mutual trust with the added benefit of sharing information and communicating quickly between its members. One such model will ideally have four to six full-time members, including a secretary with a flair for administration. A doctor, three nursing sisters and a social worker provides a balanced team, which allows in times of sickness or holiday periods enough people still to be available as a resource and to cover a 24 hour on-call system. If a team is linked to a local hospital (perhaps due to historical reasons in the planning for the team) having a consultant based there with particular responsibilities to the team can be a great advantage.

The way the team works with its consultant will evolve over time but some advantages have been learned by experience. The authority of the consultant as a back-up in requesting new resources is helpful, while his links with other consultants and the district medical team are invaluable. His knowledge about the treatment of cancer is an added resource for the team. He may also take part in the 24 hour on-call system. The more objective viewpoint of someone who is not involved in the day-to-day running of the team, when team issues are discussed can help the team decision-making process.

There may also be some disadvantages for a team to be linked to one particular hospital, when it is designed to serve a health district which may include other hospitals and resources, but, as has been said before, teams are working and being set up in many areas; their structures depend on many variable factors and the purpose of this chapter is to offer experience and ideas from a variety of teams which may be used as guidelines in the setting up of teams in the future.

An important aspect of team structure is for the team to all be using the one base from which to work. The whole ethos of the team will be different if this does not happen. The value of the informal and formal sharing of information enhancing the quality of communication between team members cannot be over-estimated, and this is achieved far more easily by the sharing of accommodation.

The first hour or so each morning can provide a time to discuss the previous day's visits or the previous night's on-call, plan, allocate new referrals, with perhaps a longer weekly or twice weekly meeting where more detailed management of patients' problems can be discussed. Time for one another is an important aspect of the team's work; being able to ask advice from one another, formally or informally, enhances the team's ability to work out policies and helps the ethos of an individual team to emerge. Providing a link between hospital and community means that the team has a considerable educative task. Not only do they need to spend time meeting hospital personnel but they also have to get to know and build relationships with community resources. Most teams have a particular catchment area from which they take referrals and in which they can visit patients at home.

The advisory, educative nature of the team means that it does not take over care of patients; its main aim is to work alongside other community or hospital resources, so they can use and develop their own skills and knowledge in the care of dying and bereaved people. It is a very sensitive area and one which sometimes offers more stress and strain to team members, than doing the work with patients. The team is really only able to work in the community with the permission of the GP and within the hospital with the agreement of hospital personnel, so the building of links and trust is of paramount importance.

The educative role of the team again depends on its structure and where its particular links are. For some teams, linked to teaching hospitals, regular teaching of nurses, medical students and social work students is already seen as the norm, for others this will be a new area of work to instigate. As individual teams establish themselves, they will work out how best to achieve their educational function; much will depend on the skill, experience and confidence of individual team members, and their ability to develop individual skills. It can be very useful to show the inter-relationship between the medical and emotional aspects of patients' needs by developing a policy of doing joint teaching sessions, so that nurse and social worker or doctor and social worker teach together, illustrating symbolically the multi-disciplinary nature of the work, showing by example how it can work in practice.

With regard to the bereavement and follow-up aspect of the work, again much will depend on the team structure, how the team develops and the numbers of people involved that require follow-up. There are various ways of handling this work. Sometimes all that is necessary is some telephone contact by the keyworker to the remaining spouse with a view to offering something at a later date at a deeper level if either he needs or will accept it. There may be the opportunity to offer group sessions to relatives who are at a similar stage of grief. Individual counselling may well be something the social worker would see as her particular role, and part of the work with the family before the patient dies is to assess the needs of a relative and to offer particular support with a view to support after the death.

In the final analysis, teams need to be aware of the needs of the bereaved, apply grief theory to each individual case and try to plan accordingly. This area of work is the one which each team will develop in its own individual way. Some teams may refer patients on to community groups and over time may need to develop resources where they have identified gaps in local resources.

There are various factors which will affect the role of a social worker within a team. One will be the way the team is structured – if its ethos is multidisciplinary in practice as well as in theory – and another will be if she is based on the same site as the rest of the team. Yet another factor will be the social worker's own experience, her perception of her role and whether it is a part-time or a full-time post.

There is by the very nature of the job some role overlap. For example, the role of counsellor is not necessarily just the social worker's. The doctors and nurses in their skilled handling and understanding of the needs of any particular patient or family, with distressing pain or symptoms, offer much support and understanding as part of their work with that particular family. Indeed, the key worker with any patient or family is often the individual who does the initial interview; it is as though a bond is formed when pain or symptoms are relieved. There is obviously a close link between physical and emotional pain and so the initial interview often acts as a catalyst, and enables the work of the team to begin.

There are, however, specific roles for the social worker within the team.

● The social worker is *a resource* for other members of the team about knowledge of local authority resources such as domiciliary services, and voluntary and community services. She should be able to advise on DHSS benefits relevant to sick patients and their families. She may also investigate adult foster schemes and more flexible ways of helping patients and families in the terminal phase of their illness; gain knowledge about any financial aid that can be applied for; develop links with British Telecom so patients can benefit from early installation of telephones, if this is necessary to enable them to stay at home as long as possible; contact the Citizens Advice Bureau to speak to the team about legal implications of various social situations where death is imminent, so all team members have this knowledge if they are the key worker with a family.

Initially the social worker may take on responsibility for gathering the information, for the use of the team as a whole; a secretary could take on the organisation of resources as time goes by.

● In an *advisory and liaison role* as the support team will service a specific area health authority which will, no doubt, be covered by various area social services offices. An important role is to liaise and link in with these colleagues, who may already be involved with patients and their families through, for example, home helps, or OTs already visiting. Meeting them and talking to them about the team's work and finding ways to work together is something very appropriately achieved by the social worker to the team, as well as acting in a consultative role if they have specific questions about any patients' or families' needs or want advice about bereavement or how to handle certain acute reactions to grief. This can involve indirect work with clients like co-ordinating effort and acting as a resource for people already trusted by patient and family.

Linking and liaising with hospital social workers in a similar way is an important aspect of the social worker's role. At least one of the social workers attached to the London terminal care support teams is linked to a social work team in a hospital. The supervision received and the value of support of social work colleagues cannot be underestimated, not only for her own professional development but for her to be reminded about the wider aspects of social work, and its management.

The social worker has an advisory role within the team, also, as a contribution to total care. With their training in human development, group and family dynamics, child care, reaction to stress, disruption of normal coping mechanisms, social workers are a resource for the team itself as well as being able to offer a contribution as previously stated, to others in the community.

● The social worker engages in *direct work with patients and family* for, while the counselling of patients may well be shared with other team members, special training in family therapy techniques, conducting family interviews and bereavement counselling are particular skills the social worker can offer to the team. Group work experience is very useful in thinking of support groups for family or bereavement groups. Generic social work experience, giving an overview of family dynamics and seeing the patient not in isolation but as part of their family group, is an aspect of social work training that can be very useful for the team in direct work with patients and their families. Experience of working with children, elderly people and the mentally ill is an added resource for the working of the team. There are also the skills in helping the team work with difficult families by, for example, giving permission to other professionals in the team to set boundaries for patients (and themselves) when their behaviour becomes childish or childlike or when they are obviously not going to change or be able to be worked with.

Using the theoretical background from social work training helps a more thorough assessment of the patient's and family's needs. Particular knowledge about loss and bereavement may help to identify certain problems and help the whole team to look at preventive work, anticipatory grieving, and so on.

Experience in marital work and an ability to offer this as part of the work a couple may wish to do in the terminal phase of an illness of one of the partners is an extremely useful resource. Then there are crisis intervention skills in being able to use the crisis to help patients and families come to a better understanding of their problems.

A role which may be more implicit than explicit is the role of "supervising" the casework being carried out by other members of the team. The nurses and doctors are often the key workers in counselling a patient or family and the advice of the social worker in the management of the case may well be crucial to its outcome; for example, it is not often appropriate to introduce a new person into a family situation if the major problem is a medical one, so advice given at that stage on how to cope with the family dynamics to whoever is involved can be seen as indirect as opposed to direct involvement but, none the less, important. At a later stage, it may be appropriate to refer the family to the social worker for particular work to be done but the sharing of cases and the overlap of roles within a multidisciplinary team which works closely together is one of the more unusual and interesting aspects of the social worker's role within the team.

● In the *teaching and educative role*, one of the first educative roles of the social worker is to help other team members to understand what a social worker can offer to the team and why. It may be the first time either doctors or nurses (or consultant) have had such close contact with a social worker. Indeed, they may have pre-conceived ideas and expectations which do not fit those of the social worker at all.

The advisory and educative role is one which develops as the job develops and as the team becomes established; teaching, however, is a very important aspect of the whole team's role and its work in the community. Some examples are contributing to the nursing and medical students' training programme, running groups on loss and bereavement for local social services departments and multi-disciplinary participants in the health authority. One team has started to organise regular workshops on all aspects of terminal care as part of its educational function.

This role can be an opportunity to develop any latent teaching skills she may have. An exciting aspect of this work can be to develop a style and pattern of education that can be used creatively with differing groups of people – the use of experiential exercises, role-play and video. The use of formal teaching methods are of questionable value, perhaps, if we are asking people to get sensitised to, learn about and internalise aspects of death and dying and its effect on patients and families.

● The social worker may have a role in *enabling, promoting and encouraging* mutual support among team members in order to start working out together the effects, if any, of working continually with death and dying. It may allow the team to begin to look at what effect, if any, it has upon all members as individuals. This may be an informal role, as part of day to day working, or structured more formally according to the desire of team members. Sometimes outside supervisors are employed to offer this form of support.

The role of the social worker, then, can be seen as a varied one, with some overlap with other team members. The need to be flexible and to perceive how roles may change and develop as a team becomes established is a very necessary skill to acquire. For example, as the number of referrals increase there will be more emphasis on bereavement, and a need to look at how the team copes with this aspect of care.

The education programme may need to be developed with research into various aspects of care. Evaluation of the team's work is necessary to improve practice. The development of volunteers as a resource for patients, with the necessary training and supervision is another possibility for the future. The idea of bringing "hospice" into the community is still relatively new and there is still much to learn to achieve a consistently high standard of care.

It is an area of work with a surprising amount of job satisfaction. If patient and family have managed to achieve the terminal phase of an illness in the way they have planned, with pain and symptoms controlled, then there is a sense of achievement and knowledge that, given the constraints of inevitable sadness and loss, there has been a job well done.

4

Teamwork in the community
Peter Pritchard

Caring for people who are at the end of their life or when they are bereaved calls for the application of a variety of skills. Some of these skills are recognised as part of the professional work of people such as nurses, social workers and doctors: lay people or alternative therapists provide other skills. The central figure, however, both as the *object* of care and as an *active participant*, is the client or patient; the person providing the main support in the community is a close second. By focussing on the client and supporter there is less temptation to regard terminal care and bereavement as a medical phenomenon, where the emphasis is almost always curative. By definition terminal care starts when medicine has "failed" to arrest the process of dying. So doctors and nurses need to change their goals from curing to caring, and mobilise support from a variety of lay and professional co-workers.

This chapter will consider teamwork in the community involving all these people. The main emphasis will be on the structure and function of teams, and how they might learn to work for the greatest benefit of the client or patient and supporter.

Cartwright, Hockey and Anderson (1973) in their classic study *Life before Death* looked at the lives and care received by a random sample of 960 adults in 12 areas in England and Wales in the year before they died. Sixty nine per cent reported "very distressing" symptoms and sixty three per cent had symptoms for a year or more. Sixty three per cent had "very distressing pain" in many cases present for a year or more. A third of those dying at home had had help from a district nurse and 13 per cent from a health visitor or other nurse. Eighty eight per cent had received a home visit from the general practitioner, and all but four per cent had had some contact with the general practitioner during the year before death. Of those living alone a third had had no visit from any official or voluntary worker, other than the GP. This survey painted a bleak picture.

Services for the dying have undoubtedly shown some improvement since the survey was done in 1969, but the situation described by the research workers was one of isolation, lack of co-ordinated professional care, and of unrelieved symptoms. The hospice movement has contributed to better pain relief and highly skilled specialist nursing care, where teamwork between staff, client and family is emphasised (Twycross 1984).

While there are now more nurses and social workers attached

to general practice, there is little or no evidence of *effective* teamwork. General practitioners now pay fewer visits to people in their homes, and consequently have to rely on other professionals or supporters to report their patients' needs to them. So how can we look at teamwork to see if it is operating effectively in the clients' and team members' interests, and how it relates to the main issues surrounding terminal care?

In terminal care much of team members' work is done alone with the client, yet co-operation is necessary – certainly between doctors, nurses and social workers – in order to define roles and role-boundaries, and to co-ordinate procedures. In this way skills will be used more appropriately, and so less wastefully.

Teamwork is an adaptive learning process in which team members affect each other – not just in articulating and maintaining professional values, but also in learning from each other and so raising their own standards of care. These peer influences are a subtle but powerful force for change, provided the milieu is constructive rather than apathetic or competitive, and that there is some perception of a common purpose and shared values. Good teamwork is reflected in the high morale of a team which can "share responsibility for outcome" even when the outcome is inevitably a sad one.

A team is defined as "a group of people who make different contributions towards the achievement of a common goal". Gilmore *et al* (1974) described the essential characteristics of teamwork as follows:

☐ The members of a team share a common purpose which binds them together and guides their actions.

☐ Each member of the team has a clear understanding of his own functions, and recognises common interests.

☐ The team works by pooling knowledge, skills, and resources and all members share responsibility for outcome.

☐ The effectiveness of the team is related to its capabilities to carry out its work and its ability to manage itself as an independent group of people.

The team must incorporate the patient/client and supporter (Pritchard 1981), and be in touch with local community networks as well as professional and lay helping agencies. In the context of this book, the patient or client would be terminally ill or bereaved, and would request or be referred for help. The professional helpers most likely to be involved in terminal illness at home would be the general practitioner and the district nurse. This is an example of an intrinsic team (Pritchard 1981) (see Figure 1).

As the tasks change, other people – lay and professional – would be involved, such as a special nurse, a hospice liaison nurse, a social worker or a lay night attendant. The basic structure of the team would remain centred on the patient and support network, each with their own special needs. If the patient is admitted to hospital, a different group of helpers takes over, but the principle of the intrinsic team should continue.

This intrinsic team is the basic building block of teamwork, but it needs mortar and reinforcement if it is to function effectively. The mortar is good communication, so that messages are passed

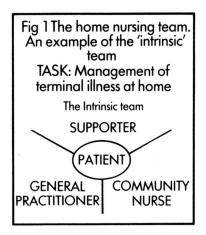

Fig 1 The home nursing team. An example of the 'intrinsic' team
TASK: Management of terminal illness at home
The Intrinsic team
SUPPORTER
PATIENT
GENERAL PRACTITIONER
COMMUNITY NURSE

speedily and the people concerned can meet often, both formally and informally. Reinforcement takes the form of regular review of mutual caseloads in order to share information and decide on action.

Community-based teams can help in using limited resources effectively, in evaluating outcomes and in maintaining morale of team members. They would cover the whole range of team-work, not just one aspect such as terminal care. This is an important distinction, between a centrally managed "vertical" organisation of services with a narrow range of tasks, and a "horizontal" organisation where inter-disciplinary cross-linking is more important than the hierarchical lines of control. Herein lies a major source of conflict in teamwork. For success there must be a high level of fieldwork autonomy and flexibility which is negated by managerial control from above. Managerial support and sensitive monitoring are needed, but detailed scrutiny and control of field workers' time, tasks and decisions will make teamwork ineffective if not impossible (see Figure 2).

Within primary health care, the teams consist mainly of doctors, nurses and lay staff. Doctors tend to assume a lot of authority, both as employers of lay staff and practice nurses, and from traditional hospital-based relationships between doctors and nurses. This authority is being strongly questioned by health visitors and district nurses who are becoming increasingly autonomous.

Social workers have never accepted that doctors have over-riding authority, nor do they accept a medical model of caring, so relationships between the primary health care team and social workers can be more difficult to develop. This is no reason to be put off, but rather to look into ways of developing team working so that it is task-oriented, effective, and satisfying for staff and patients/clients.

The Seebohm report (1968) envisaged attachment of social workers to health centres on a fairly long-term basis, and some progress has been made in this direction. The Barclay report (1982), in contrast, had very little to say on the subject of co-operation between social and health workers. But now there is objective evidence that such co-operation does result in improved patient care (for example, Wilkinson 1982), which reinforces the firm belief of many general practitioners that close co-operation is essential (for example, Butrym and Horder 1987). Working as a co-ordinated team can ensure that the number of visitors to a client's home can be kept to a minimum, so that the helpers are more likely to be familiar and trusted.

The organisational structure in which primary health care and

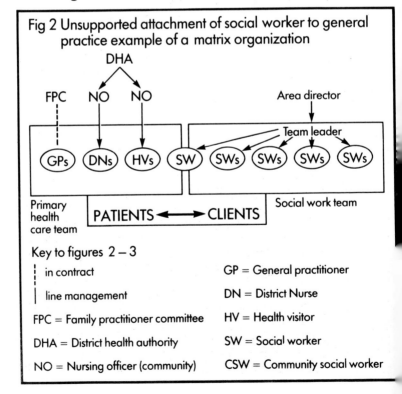

Fig 2 Unsupported attachment of social worker to general practice example of a matrix organization

Key to figures 2 – 3

┊ in contract
│ line management
FPC = Family practitioner committee
DHA = District health authority
NO = Nursing officer (community)

GP = General practitioner
DN = District Nurse
HV = Health visitor
SW = Social worker
CSW = Community social worker

social work operate at field level is a crucial factor for success. Several patterns have emerged, for example:

1 Attachment of a junior social worker part-time to a group practice without accepting direct referrals.
2 As above but accepting direct referrals.
3 Incorporating a full-time (preferably senior) social worker in the primary health care team.
4 Social work team and primary health care team sharing the same (or contiguous) premises with regular meetings.
5 Separately recruited and managed branch of social work service working in health centres, with a senior and junior social worker in every large centre.

The first model is the most brittle, and almost doomed to failure from the start. To gain acceptance in a health care team the social worker must accept referrals, and have a reasonable level of autonomy in decision making, which implies a weakening of links with the social work team and hierarchy that is not always acceptable. But unless this nettle is grasped, and managers and team leaders accept a supportive and educational rather than a managerial role, interdisciplinary teamworking is very difficult, and the attached social worker is put under considerable strain.

The third model can be highly successful if there is flexibility on both sides, with the social worker becoming a valued and influential member of a more broadly based health and social welfare team. Each professional group stands to gain from co-operation, and this reinforces their commitment to client-oriented team working.

The fourth model depends on adjacent location of the two teams and active co-operation, and has worked well (in the author's experience) over many years. The method is flexible and allows staff changes to occur without too much disruption of co-operation. A team-oriented culture develops in the organisation which is a good milieu for new staff and trainees to gain experience of team working and inter-team co-operation. As well as the social work and the primary health care teams, we must consider the community nursing team, the hospice team as well as volunteer groups, all of which need to integrate their care for the individual patient or client.

A branch of social work separate from community and hospital social work is the model adopted by Strathclyde Regional Council (1981), that is standing the test of time (Leach 1987), and is popular among social and health workers. It relies on the large investment in health centres to cover the main centres of population in Strathclyde. This model is illustrated in Figure 3 (from Pritchard 1983).

Methods of developing multidisciplinary teamwork have

been worked out in industry and have been found to be equally effective in primary health care and social work settings, although few examples of their application in the UK have been recorded. The team development model was pioneered in the USA by Richard Beckhard (1972), Rubin & Beckhard (1972), and has been used successfully in the UK for development of nursing, primary health care, social work and management teams.

Team development can first be tackled separately in primary health care and social work teams, and then joint team development attempted in the workplace. This strategy is easiest to implement and should produce fairly quick results, but requires motivation to work well together, as well as the investment of time and energy. Team members' own skills in group working can be used. However, strong nerves are needed, as the first meeting or two can be explosive. Team development meetings should initially be separate from ordinary meetings, so that there is a clear focus on review and development with time set aside for it.

An alternative strategy for "in-house" learning is to use an educational package such as that developed by Rubin *et al* (1975), with or without an outside consultant or facilitator. The program is expected to take seven three-hour sessions.

A third strategy is the one commonly used in the UK, in which interested individuals from different settings attend joint sessions away from the workplace. These sessions may help to improve attitudes, teach the skills of working together and motivate teamwork, but the methods then have to be applied in the work setting, which means implementing the first or second strategy described above. So to expect much progress from such meetings alone is unrealistic.

Like any other educational intervention, evaluation against

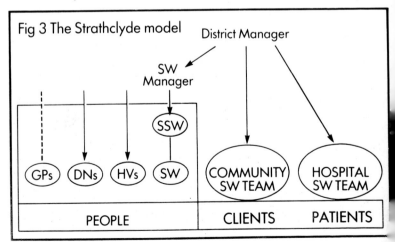

Fig 3 The Strathclyde model

objectives is essential, but in a field like team development, or teamworking in general, evaluation has not been given the attention it deserves. Evaluation of the effectiveness of teamwork is possible using process measures such as time-delay analysis, and outcome measures such as patient and staff satisfaction, but in terminal care and bereavement outcome measures are more likely to be subjective (implicit), for example client satisfaction or the assessment of quality of care, or of life. These implicit criteria may be valuable in that they measure, however crudely, qualities that are central to professional work (Donabedian 1981).

High morale has been mentioned as a characteristic of good teamwork, and this can be monitored subjectively. When team members learn to know and trust one another, they become less concerned with role boundaries and develop more role flexibility, which can also be assessed. Firm conclusions based on research are scanty in this field, so evaluation based on experience has to take its place.

Many of the foregoing arguments have favoured generic teamworking of a high standard, which can then be applied to a wide range of tasks, of which terminal care and bereavement are perhaps the most taxing of all. But teamworking will be of no avail if knowledge and skills are missing or attitudes are negative or contradictory.

Knowledge of terminal care and bereavement can be shared by making texts available in the unit which all staff can use. Examples are Kübler-Ross (1974), Murray Parkes (1972), Saunders (1984), Spilling (1986), Twycross (1984) and Twycross & Lack (1983). Lunchtime meetings with a suitable audio or videotape to focus discussion can be very helpful. Visits from hospice staff, or members of mutual help groups like CRUSE are valuable.

The point of transition, when care becomes terminal, may be seen differently by the doctor, who perhaps has medical reports which have not been told in full to the patient, and who would tend to follow a "worst-case" scenario, while trying to keep up the patient's spirits with optimism. The patient, in isolation, may have to penetrate this smokescreen of false optimism and partial truth in order to reach a conclusion that death is certain, and that the doctor's optimism cannot be trusted. Perhaps the patient should not be put in this position, by ensuring that truth is maintained. This is more likely to occur with a team who share high professional and personal values, and who discuss such things openly, and maintain the client's integrity and dignity.

But should there be a sudden change of mode at the point when the threat to life is perceived as certain? Is this transition point certain or clear cut, with two alternatives – life or death? Perhaps doctors should remind themselves that life is finite and death a certainty, so that the change from optimism to a sense of failure is less of a shock for patient and doctor. The caring has to continue till death (and afterwards for those bereaved), and the same core team is still involved. So what might serve the client's needs best is a flexible and versatile team approach that can tackle a wide range of tasks, rather than have specific therapists for specific tasks, working in isolation. This more generic and continuing approach makes it more likely that team members are in touch with, and have the confidence of potential clients. But a generic approach cannot succeed if team members lack the specialist knowledge and skills described in other chapters, nor if they fail to call on specialist help when needed.

Coping with bereavement is an important task for team members. They need to know not only how to lessen the bereaved person's suffering, or to prevent a slide into ill-health and premature death, but also how to help team members themselves cope with their feelings of failure and grief. Repeated visits to grieving relatives may be very stressful, and the temptation to let them lapse when other work presses can only be resisted by an agreed system of follow-up and mutual support from team members.

One helpful procedure is to keep a register of all deaths in the practice, with date and address. All staff can have access to it, and the practice manager could ensure that people who need to know are told. Anniversary reminders can be given to all staff involved in bereavement follow-up.

Sharing the visiting between – say – GP and health visitor or social worker can reduce their stress. Progress can be discussed and plans shared. The two workers can, when appropriate, adopt different roles, with one as the comforter and the other as the realist. Sharing care can also result in less dependence on tranquillising drugs and sleeping tablets which doctors tend to prescribe when at a loss to help people's intolerable grief.

A social worker who has been in contact with the client or family before death will certainly want to keep contact going, in concert with other team members. Even when not involved, the social worker can help other team members – particularly inexperienced ones – come to terms with their own feelings in the face of death and bereavement. In a well-knit team, the social worker may naturally assume a key role of informal counsellor to the team.

Grief in the face of terminal illness, death and bereavement can spread beyond the immediate family circle and affect whole communities. This can happen in the event of a local disaster, or when someone dies who is much loved in the neighbourhood – particularly when a child dies in tragic circumstances. Members of the health and social care teams have close links with many community networks, and are particularly well placed to help with neighbourhood grief reactions. The school nurse or health visitor may have a valuable role in helping children to grieve (Carter 1986).

Teamwork does not happen automatically, even when people work together in a suitably designed organisation. Active development of team working is needed, using well-established educational methods.

Teamwork must be focussed by sharing values and aims, and roles must be clearly understood by all, but interpreted flexibly according to circumstances. The technical content of the work must be taught, with monitoring of process and outcome. All in all a daunting task! But the benefits in better care and client satisfaction, as well as in improved staff satisfaction and morale, are likely to justify the effort and commitment needed.

Barclay committee *Social Workers: Their Role and Tasks*. National Institute for Social Work. 1982.

Beckhard, R "Organisational issues in team delivery of health care", *Milbank Memorial Fund Quarterly*. **50**, 287–316. 1972.

Butrym, Z and Horder, J *Health, Doctors and Social Workers*. Routledge and Kegan Paul. 1983.

Carter, P "Helping children to grieve", *Nursing Times* (*Community Outlook*, 16–20) 1986.

Cartwright, A, Hockey, L and Anderson, R *Life before Death*. Routledge and Kegan Paul. 1973.

Donabedian, A "Advantages and disadvantages of explicit criteria for assessing the quality of health care", *Milbank Memorial Fund Quarterly*. **59**, No 1 99–106. 1981.

Gilmore, M *et al The Work of the Nursing Team in General Practice*. Council for the Education and Training of Health Visitors. 1974.

Kübler-Ross, E *Questions and Answers on Death and Dying*. Collier Macmillan, New York. 1974.

Leach, M Personal communication to the author. 1987.

Parkes, C M *Bereavement*. Penguin. 1972.

Pritchard, P M M *Manual of Primary Health Care* (2nd edn). Oxford University Press. 1981.

Pritchard, P M M "A view from general practice", in *The Barclay Report: Papers from a Consultation Day*. National Institute for Social Work Paper No 15. 1983.

Rubin, I M and Beckhard, R "Factors influencing the effectiveness of health teams", *Milbank Memorial Fund Quarterly*. **50**, Part 2. 317–35. 1972.

Rubin, I M *et al Improving the Co-ordination of Care. A Programme for Health Team Development*. Ballinger. Cambridge, Mass. 1975.

Saunders, C M *The Management of Terminal Disease* (2nd edn). Edward Arnold. 1984.

Seebohm committee *Report of the Committee on Local Authority and Allied*

Personal Social Services. Cmnd 3703. HMSO. 1968.

Spilling, R (ed) *Terminal Care at Home.* Oxford University Press. 1986.

Strathclyde Regional Council *Social Work in Health Centres. Results of a Survey Undertaken in Eleven Centres in Strathclyde.* 1981.

Twycross, R G *A Time to Die.* Christian Medical Fellowship Publications. 1984.

Twycross, R G & Lack, S A *Symptom Control in Far-Advanced Cancer: Pain Relief.* Pitman. 1983.

Wilkinson, G "Social Work: Effective or Affective?" *British Medical Journal.* **284** 1959–60. 1982

The author wishes to acknowledge gratefully the help he has received from John Horder, Moira Leitch, Jenny Littlewood and Donald Mungall.

5

Setting up and running a bereavement service

Elizabeth Earnshaw-Smith

D r Colin Murray Parkes (1975) speaks of bereavement as a psycho-social transition requiring from those who would help time, empathy and trust, and he maintains that the care of the bereaved should be a communal activity. A volunteer bereavement counselling service would seem to serve such a purpose. It sets help for the bereaved firmly within the sphere of the community (Hirsch 1978), within the capability of lay helpers, neighbours, visitors, counsellors. Furthermore, it provides a channel through which an understanding of loss and bereavement can be conveyed, and ideas about ways of helping disseminated to ordinary people. It spreads a confidence that painful, dreaded happenings can be survived, that it is possible to approach and stay close to anguish and depression without it destroying the sufferer or his relative, friend or neighbour.

Social work has long been the profession most concerned with loss – loss of personal identity in psychiatric illness, loss of child and loss of parents through reception into local authority care, loss of home for elderly people in residential care, loss of independence and dignity in the handicapped, loss of coping ability and control in "problem" families, loss of freedom for offenders. This wealth of experience in the field of loss makes social workers familiar with the skills necessary for working with the bereaved and the profession most suited to setting up and running a bereavement service, handing on their experience and skills to those who can help and enable without stigmatising.

However, it is important to tread warily, to proceed slowly, to take stock frequently, because we are asking lay people to do something difficult – to be where the public don't want to be, in the presence of anguish which can sometimes arouse strangely painful feelings and memories in the helper.

In setting up and running a bereavement service we need to consider: preparing the ground; selecting counsellors and rejecting those who are unsuitable; training; and running the service.

Preparing the ground
A bereavement service must be wanted. It must be structured to meet real needs and it can only survive if there are realistic

expectations on both sides (Johnston 1978).

The following questions need to be asked, researched and answered before it is wise to go ahead:

☐ On what grounds has it been decided that a bereavement service is needed? What kind and how great are the needs? Are there other agencies in the field who give support to the bereaved so that another service might lead to duplication or confusion? To get to know other agencies at an early stage can be invaluable in enhancing opportunities for co-operative effort, collaboration, economy and good relations. Agencies working with specific groups such as elderly people or young mothers or providing a service such as lunch clubs can take over where a bereavement counsellor leaves off in helping a bereaved person to socialise again, or provide opportunities for them to become helpers themselves.

☐ There are important people in a community whose co-operation and help must be sought. Local firms, rotary clubs, charities may be pleased to give financial help to launch a project. Clergy and ministers and those doing regular cemetery or crematorium duty can be important in both making referrals and giving additional support to some bereaved people. Ward or casualty sisters in hospitals can be encouraged to make prompt and sensitive referrals. The mortician in a hospital has a very important task in conducting grief-stricken families to see the body of their loved one; but he rarely has training or on-going support in the use of this occasion to enable people to touch and handle the dead, to pause for as long as they need for the truth to sink in and to begin to get over their shock and, in their own time, to say goodbye and let go. The mortician must know about the bereavement service.

☐ What are the class structure and ethnic groupings in the area? It is sometimes unacceptable to introduce bereavement counsellors from a rival community, and counsellors from different ethnic groups can best help their own group while at the same time they will bring a wide understanding of cross-cultural patterns of bereavement to the service.

☐ Who will be in charge of the service and to whom is that person accountable? Which decisions have to be referred to a higher authority? How much freedom does the leader in fact have and in what areas? If a volunteer makes a mistake of judgement who will stand by him? Who will be responsible for advertising in the press or reimbursing volunteers for their expenses?

☐ To whom is the service to be directed? Bereavement counselling is time consuming. Any one person having difficulty with their bereavement may require weeks, months or even one to two years of faithful visiting. It is hard to know how much time will be needed by a bereaved person until work has begun.

Because it is difficult to turn down those asking for help, it is wise to start by setting up a pilot service to a limited group – perhaps for the children's unit or the geriatric unit of a hospital, or one parish in a community, or for those whose relatives have committed suicide, or for families of cancer patients, or those who have had a stillbirth. Is there a national society of which your project could become a member and from which it could draw experience, expertise and resources?

☐ Are there people who oppose or are doubtful of the need for a service? It is very important to face their concerns with them before starting, and where at all possible to come to some resolution or compromise. A service can be undermined by those who feel their legitimate worries have not been understood or taken into consideration.

☐ What will be the relationship between the service and the general practitioners in the area? Even if general practitioners do not make referrals to the service, counsellors may need to consult a bereaved person's doctor and will need to feel that the service which they represent is known about, understood and respected by the doctor.

☐ Who is going to select, train and supervise the counsellors? If a social worker, how will this affect her relationship with her agency? If a voluntary services co-ordinator, will there be an opportunity for specialist training in this field? Difficult decisions must be made regarding bereaved people at special risk, or about volunteer under particular stress, or entrenched in a complex relationship with a family.

☐ How will referrals be made and who will turn down unsuitable referrals, and when and how? How will numbers be limited to those which can be realistically handled, taking into consideration the overall volunteer time available, travelling time, recording time and the types of volunteers working in the service? There are factors which seem to complicate bereavement and the process of grieving. These may include lack of community or spiritual support; actual or feared loss of home; children or adolescents in the immediate family; the presence of recurrent life crises; dependent family members; and other such matters. It may be wise to limit help initially to those who have these or some of these additional difficulties.

☐ What factors will determine whether a bereaved person can be referred to a volunteer or if professional help is required?

☐ From whom can expert or professional advice be obtained at short notice or over a weekend?

☐ If the service is part of a social service department or

hospital, the preliminary discussions with management and staff are of great importance. What kind of expectations have they of the service? Such expectations must coincide precisely with the service provided, or the staff and the bereaved will be disappointed and confused. When working with professional staff it is therefore important to discover their aims, standards, ambitions, how they feel about volunteers working with their patients, or their clients. What is their previous experience of volunteers? Can they accept a bereavement counsellor's work as an extension of their own? Misapprehensions and fears must be dealt with before they have their undermining effect on a new service, and staff need reassurance about the calibre of bereavement counsellors who will be working with them.

Selection of counsellors

Bereavement counselling consists of understanding and facilitating a normal process. But it also involves carrying the anxieties and fears of a community or institution regarding death, loss and mortality. Unlike many kinds of voluntary work, the bereavement counsellor is unlikely to get immediate satisfaction. We are asking volunteers to visit someone they have not met before, often to visit alone, to stay with depression through weeks or months, to see little change without getting too discouraged, to contain angry feelings and occasional angry outbursts. The family want their dead returned to them, and the effort of talking about their loss is exceedingly painful and hard work and they may be reluctant.

We are therefore looking for people with sensitivity, warmth, realism, courage and persistence, common sense and self-confidence. Tolerance of frustration, ambiguity and disappointment are indispensable. We need people who can allow, without projection, the reawakening of their own painful feelings of loss. Above all, we are looking for people who can listen with total attention, who can withhold from giving their own personal interpretations or advice, can sustain silence as an acknowledgment that words are inadequate, can identify with helplessness. On an intellectual level, we need counsellors who are capable of grasping theoretical concepts and understanding some of the complex reactions of the bereaved to the experience they are going through.

Selection must therefore be rigorous (Johnston 1978). It is not only the service but the volunteer and his family who have to live with the stress and tension which can be caused by an unwise decision. Many people give as their reason for wanting to be bereavement counsellors, their own experience of bereavement. This, if worked through to some resolution, has the potential for enabling counsellors to be understanding, realistic

56

and helpful. But for others their interest in training arises out of a need to work through their own grief; they are still unconsciously searching for relief or support (Garfield & Jenkins 1981–2) and it is sometimes difficult to distinguish the potential helpers from those still needing help for themselves. Such people have great difficulty in opening up painful areas for discussion with the bereaved and too many "blind spots" which hinder effective counselling (Worden 1983). It is wise to make a rigid rule that no-one is accepted for training within two years of a major loss or crisis. But even so, unresolved grief can linger for many years and it is important to look closely for signs of such continuing pain at interview.

Interviewing is time-consuming, and turning down applicants is difficult. A clear and specific advertisement may therefore be helpful in attracting suitable volunteers who may then be asked to complete a simple application form. This will convey to the applicant a little more about the kind of person the service is looking for, test out their seriousness in pursuing their application, exclude some at this stage who are clearly unsuitable and provide points on which to focus at interview. References may also be asked for.

An interview must not develop into a chat. Its success depends on the disciplined preparation of purposeful, indirect and open-ended questions. The interviewer will be watching and listening for clear, direct answers; but also for emotional undertones and non-verbal communication, trying to see the real person behind the inevitably nervous exterior. It can be helpful to have two interviewers working together to increase their objectivity, and a professional consultant to interview separately. A joint decision to accept or reject an applicant can then be made which feels safer to the interviewers and fairer to the interviewees.

Interviews are hard work and it is important to keep to time as there is much to discover. What motivates her? What sustains her? Would she be able to absorb and adopt new ideas, techniques and skills? What are her attitudes, prejudices and interests? How has she handled losses and crises in herself, her family, or in friends? Would she fit into and be able to draw support from a group of counsellors in training and supervision?

A group discussion for applicants can further clarify these issues. Topics might include a situation they may fear they will encounter as counsellors such as aggressiveness, suicide, alcoholism or the place of religion in counselling; or they could be asked to discuss a video, role play or a case presentation of a family bereavement. Some organisations, such as Relate, use aptitude and personality tests as well as interviewing.

A probationary or trial period is always reassuring for selector and applicant, providing an opportunity to test out inclination and aptitude for this kind of work. Perhaps a period covering the training course and three months as a counsellor. At the end of the period there must be a formal review and a clear decision made which gives as much credence to the applicant's self-selection as to the selectors' choice of the applicant for bereavement counselling. This acceptance must be an event shared by the whole bereavement counselling team. In this way the new counsellor feels a full member of the group from the beginning and recognition is given to the particular gifts and qualities she brings. This will prevent her being deskilled by the selection process and enable her to work with confidence as a full member of a supportive team and with the backing of its leader and professional consultant.

Rejection

Rejection is the most difficult part of selection. It may take place after receiving the application, at interview, after the group selection, during training or after a while at work. It may be a decision by the applicant or counsellor that this is not the kind of voluntary work for her, or by the leader of the service (Johnston 1978).

In considering rejection we must be clear why it is necessary to be selective. It is so that volunteers are used responsibly and the bereaved are given effective help, avoiding any additional pain caused by insensitivity or intrusiveness. An applicant who does not make selectors feel they could trust her with their own grief may not inspire confidence in the bereaved or the agencies and individuals who would otherwise refer bereaved people to the service.

It is important to be on the look out throughout the selection procedure and the early days of counselling for clues to acceptable and face-saving reasons for rejection. The whole process should enable an applicant to form her own opinion regarding her suitability as a counsellor, and provide opportunities for her to choose an alternative type of voluntary work if necessary.

It should be the responsibility of the leader of the service and those sharing in the interviewing to be aware of alternative openings for voluntary work, giving realistic advice so that the applicant will not be turned down again. Some will find their own ways of leaving: for others it is kinder to give a clear, unmistakable "no". Always it is important to enable applicants or counsellors to leave with a good grace, having clarified with the leader some of the positives in themselves or in their work which they can take on with them to a different task.

Training

The most valuable resource of a bereavement project is its counsellors and all they bring with them of satisfying relationships and life experience, of tried ways of handling disappointments, crises and losses in themselves, their families and friends. They also bring with them optimism, a belief that there is a way through, together with all the individual qualities for which they have been selected. The dilemma for the bereavement project leader is how to train these counsellors without deskilling them or devaluing the personal contributions they bring to the service (Volunteer Centre 1977). Volunteers must be trained primarily to use themselves; but their enthusiasm to learn "techniques" and to find "answers" can seduce a leader into teaching as if such solutions to human problems existed.

Training sessions must be disciplined, encouraging, stimulating and supportive. A group which has been securely welded together through a training programme will provide the necessary support to its members when they start work; a group in which they can share, criticise constructively, relax and enjoy themselves.

Before designing a training programme it is helpful to consider certain practical issues:

☐ The financial resources available will determine where the course is to be held, to what extent it can draw on specialists in the field who will be paid for their teaching commitment, or on those who live or work in the area and could give of their time and expertise.

☐ The size of the group should be such that trainees can get to know one another and share together. It is often better to start with a small, cohesive group of counsellors who can be given plenty of on-going support and supervision after training.

☐ The room in which they are to have their training sessions must also be considered carefully. Learning takes place more readily in comfortable, bright, pleasant and quiet surroundings. It is a help to have space so that people can discuss in twos and threes or small groups or do role plays. Access to facilities for audio-visual aids is a great asset.

A training programme must achieve a balance between theory and practice. Theory alone tends to produce counsellors who intellectualise problems, lose their spontaneity and become over-anxious about "saying the right thing". Theory must be constantly demonstrated in practice through the use of videos, films and, most importantly, through simple role play or sculpting. This enables trainees to experience how it feels on both sides of the counselling relationship, to try out different ways of conveying and eliciting feelings, to observe non-verbal as well as verbal communication.

Trainees often express anxiety about helping certain categories, such as the bereaved person who is withdrawn and finds it hard to speak; the person who can't stop talking; the person who fears that once they cry they will not be able to stop; the person with suicidal thoughts; or the person who has resorted to drink to blot out his pain and sorrow. Such situations simulated in rôle play will then feel familiar when encountered on a visit. In this way, learning is rapid, confidence is increased and theory is transmitted into practice. It is, however, very important that after every role play ample opportunity is provided for each person to assume again his own identity and to discuss the role play as a counsellor.

Trainees need a manageable reading list which contains the theory of loss, bereavement and counselling, biographical books about bereavement and also books which they can in turn give to bereaved people (including children) to read. It is always helpful if books read can be reviewed and discussed during training sessions. Because many volunteers will have little time to give outside the sessions it may be helpful to ask each trainee to read and then review one book from each section. In a similar way it may be helpful during the course for each trainee to present a short paper on a relevant subject of their choice such as bereaved parents, the loss of a spouse, violent death, suicide, depression or anger in bereavement.

Subjects which might helpfully be covered in training sessions include the human need for attachment and the consequent crisis of loss, normal symptoms of grief and symptoms requiring specialist treatment. Different experiences of bereavement may be shared within the group or studied on film or video. Ways of helping with depression, anger and guilt must be discovered, and some of the practical problems which the bereaved face must be addressed. The effect of a bereavement for members of a family each at different ages and stages of the life cycle must be understood, as well as the tasks of mourning to be addressed by each on their journey through bereavement. Most importantly ways of ending each interview and of ending a course of visits must be practised. Endings are memorable as they mirror bereavement itself and can provide an opportunity to summarise progress and plan the future.

Bereavement counselling has been said to be "building a bridge to the future" (Volunteer Centre 1977). A training course must help volunteers identify and build on their own strengths and resources so that they can in turn enable the bereaved to do the same.

Running the service

Having selected and trained a group of volunteers the leader must now maintain the enjoyment and stimulation they have experienced in training sessions, continuing to provide opportunities for learning, sharing and discussing their work (Volunteer Centre 1977). Supervision sessions should be regular, probably fortnightly, and attendance should be a firm commitment asked of every member. The sessions need to be varied in content giving each volunteer an opportunity to describe their first visit to a family and report on subsequent visits. In discussing these visits new insights will be gained and new ways of working and looking at situations will be explored.

Keeping up to date with new thinking and developments in the field of counselling and bereavement must also be included. New films or videos can be seen and books reviewed. Related subjects such as marital strains, the special needs of children, sexual needs and cultural variations in mourning may be discussed with specialists in these fields, or using expertise within the group. In this way each counsellor's contribution is maximised and his skills improved and extended; this is the reward he is looking for.

The work of bereavement counsellors is greatly facilitated and sharpened if they are given a form on which to record their visits. Otherwise, because of their anxiety, counsellors tend to write copious notes which only serve to increase the pressure on their time and make for confused reporting at supervision sessions. The drawing of family trees often done with the bereaved acts as an easy shorthand way of conveying much detailed information and has a powerful and helpful visual impact on the bereaved person or family. Perhaps most importantly, such a form provides the counsellor with a disciplined way of committing his thoughts and concerns about the bereaved person to paper, setting out a plan of immediate action or future contact. This enables him to disengage himself from anxieties which might otherwise stay with him when he returns to his own home and family.

A cross-referenced system of storing information regarding counsellors and their clients is vital. A leader must be able to find quickly in response to enquiries by the bereaved or those concerned about them the names, addresses and telephone numbers of counsellors and of clients, their family doctor, social worker, minister or other close family or community support. Photographic or carbon copies of counsellors' notes on their visits to clients may also be kept. (These are confidential and must be kept securely. Volunteers and clients have a right to expect high professional and ethical standards in this respect.)

Referrals to the service require careful consideration before deciding on the most appropriate action to be taken:

☐ If there are no family or friends around at the time of death a bereavement counsellor needs to make contact at an early stage. It may be necessary to accompany the bereaved person to his home after a death and help to settle him for the night, or accompany him to the registrar, funeral director and perhaps the funeral.

☐ Where there are family and friends it is better to delay visiting, thus encouraging family members to take responsibility for one another, and increase family cohesion. When neighbours and family are withdrawing and beginning to expect the bereaved to be "normal" help may be most needed, probably one to three months after the death.

☐ The decision as to who should be counselled in a family is an important one. For instance, a counsellor can split a potentially supportive relationship by seeing the next of kin alone. Conversely, a family conflict can be intensified if the counsellor insists on seeing the family together when some members are rightly struggling for normal privacy and independence.

☐ Some people withdraw in depression after bereavement and a counsellor must reach out to them. Others need to take the initiative themselves and be given a name and telephone number to contact. This may be weeks, months or even years later. Counsellors cannot force themselves on the bereaved, and must not undermine independence.

Case load management is an important aspect of the leader's task. The success of a service and the efficiency of its counsellors depend on the leader balancing the demands of the service with the fluctuating pressures on individual counsellors in their personal lives. It may be a family crisis, or moving to a new home, the younger counsellors may have to cope with children on school holidays, or retired counsellors may have periods when they are involved in looking after frail or sick relatives. At these times they may need to have a temporary break or their caseload lightened. The pressure of referrals to the service should never be passed on to the counsellors but must be absorbed and dealt with by the leader. It is better not to accept a referral than to give inadequate help. Instead, perhaps GP, social worker, church or volunteer agency might be asked to give help until a counsellor becomes available.

To begin with, counsellors tend to close their cases too quickly wanting to move on to others. This reflects their fear of intruding, going too deep, finding more problems than they can handle, or facing the pain of staying with a depressed person who feels stuck and despairing. The counsellor most needs the encouragement and support of the supervision sessions at these times to enable him to stay with the bereaved to convey comfort, security and hope. From time to time the counsellor may need to review progress with his client remembering to recall difficulties resolved as well as resources discovered, setting new goals for their grief work together.

The ending of a contract with family or bereaved person needs to be carefully thought out as this is in fact another bereavement. Supervision can help here by role playing a final interview to try out different ways of handling the situation.

A supervision time is also a good opportunity to work out how to encourage a client or family to seek professional help when this is needed. The process of clarifying for the counsellors the limits of their responsibility is always important and should be related to the cases they are working with.

Alternative ways of working can extend the usefulness of a service. A regular (perhaps monthly or quarterly) informal social may provide the only opportunity for the more unselfconfident or housebound to start socialising again. Here they will find everyone in the same position as themselves – alone, sad, diffident. Eventually some of these people may take over the running of the social and will organise other activities. The social thus becomes a place where those who have been helped may begin to become helpers.

Others may be searching for or have found a religious faith in their loss. For them a religious service gives a ritualised opportunity to remember, to let go and to start a new life. Some crematoria and churches cater for this kind of need.

Small therapeutic groups of short duration (perhaps 10 weekly 1½ hour sessions) seem to be another useful way of helping bereaved people work through their grief quickly and thoroughly. Because of their recent and traumatic common experience and their need for support these groups gel very quickly in one or two sessions. Here they discover that in the midst of their sorrow they can be givers as well as receivers. They discover, too, that the strange and frightening symptoms which sometimes seem even to threaten their sanity are common to all bereaved people and are but a passing phase. The ending of the group can be an opportunity for the members to work together on another shared bereavement. This arouses again much of the pain of loss; but this time enabling them to work through it with friends. Some members of the group may go on to find their own self-help activities in the community after the group ends. The most effective groups are understandably those which unite people who have sustained a common loss, such as a spouses' group, a parents' group or a siblings' group. They need to be run by two group leaders, one of whom should have training and experience in running small groups. Powerful feelings and deep distress can be released in them and a sense of control and containment is important. Furthermore, there are times when powerful negative emotions can be expressed in veiled terms or displaced onto other people or situations; a leader must feel confident to use these feelings in the group, otherwise they build up leaving a sense of bitterness and unresolved guilt. A well-run group can support people through periods of deep depression and allow discussion around previously unacknowledged fears.

As a bereavement service develops the helped will gradually

become helpers in their family or neighbourhood, and bereavement counsellors with increasing experience, skill and clarity will be able to speak about their work and teach others also.

Parkes, Colin Murray *Bereavement: Studies of Grief in Adult Life*. Penguin. 1975.

Hirsch, F *Social Limits to Growth*. Routledge & Kegan Paul. 1978.

Johnston, D *Working with Volunteers – Recruitment and Selection*. Volunteer Centre. 1978.

Garfield, C A & Jenkins, G J *Stress and coping of volunteers counselling the dying and bereaved. Omega*. p. 12, 1–13. 1981–2.

Worden, J W *Grief Counselling and Grief Therapy*. Tavistock. 1983.

Murphy, G *Working with Volunteers: Training*. Volunteer Centre. 1977.

Dyne, G (Ed) *Bereavement Visiting*. King Edward Hospital Fund for London. 1981.

6

The future of the hospice
Gillian Ford

The changing use of the word hospice during the last 20 years is a reflection of the diverse developments in care of the dying during that period. In the UK and abroad the term "hospice" has come to have increasing significance, describing not only bricks and mortar, but also an attitude (hospice approach or hospice philosophy), or a group of people ("hospice care team"), not associated with any in-patient unit. "Hospice medicine" is difficult to define although most who work in this field would perhaps express it as both the science of symptom control and the art of caring for patients as whole individuals and as members of families.

HOSPICE – THE PATIENTS
Saunders (1976) has pointed out that "treatment of terminal cancer is often preoccupied with the disease process and too little concerned with the special problems of the individual patient". The hospice approach seeks to redress that imbalance, to concentrate not on the inoperable or ineradicable but on symptoms that can be ameliorated and problems, whatever they consist of, which can be sorted out. By so doing individuals are enabled to be themselves and to live until the end.

Clearly there is no reason why those working in the hospice field, whether in a purpose-built unit or a support team, should have a monopoly of this approach. Nor is there any reason why only those patients with terminal malignant disease should receive specialist services.

The genesis of the present hospice movement when it started in the UK in the '60s was the neglect of patients with distressing symptoms for whom it was thought "nothing more could be done". These were usually patients with cancer and the skills in symptom control which have developed since then have been related particularly to end stage cancer. Although many hospices admit a few patients with other diagnoses (for instance, those with motor neurone disease) cancer remains by far the most frequent cause of the symptoms and other problems which lead to a referral (Hospice Information Service 1987). Whether this will continue to be the pattern is difficult to predict but there are some factors which suggest that hospice care will continue to be concentrated mainly on patients with cancer.

The first of these is that the expertise to be found in the hospice movement is based on both experience and research in terminal malignant disease. Motor neurone disease is the only other diagnosis where the number of patients cared for is such as to provide an appropriate knowledge base from which to offer a *specialist* service.

Second, the proportion of patients with terminal malignant disease who die in a hospice or continuing care unit or at home, but with a home care team alongside the usual domiciliary services in support, is small – only perhaps 10–15 per cent of the total deaths from this cause. However even this small proportion is a significant load in terms of numbers. It has been estimated that between 20,000 and 40,000 patients (*Lancet* 1986; Ford 1986) receive such services in their last few months of life and the impression is that there is overloading rather than any spare capacity to take on patients with other diagnoses and other needs.

Third, many of the units and teams are in receipt of substantial sums from cancer societies and some have had sizable legacies in recognition of their work with cancer. Most have developed with substantial community support for the prime objective of caring for patients with terminal malignant disease and their admission policies and council membership naturally reflect this now and are likely to continue to do so.

Fourth, the hospice approach now attracts substantial professional interest and support as well as public support. This is encouraging as it would be understandable if the reverse were true. Hospice staff might be suspect if they were thought to profess only that they were simply more caring or more loving than NHS colleagues, or that they had a monopoly of the secret of communication, or that they were in possession of some arcane skills which they alone could practise. On the contrary, the openness of the hospices, the existence of similar specialist units within the NHS and the advisory role of specialist nurses within the community have all lent credence to acceptance of the principles that have been promulgated. In addition the teaching programmes in which many are involved have been strengthened by painstaking clinical studies and research. Recognition of the validity of the hospice approach by medical, nursing and social work bodies has accompanied growing public awareness of the limitations of a curative approach to cancer. Increasingly individuals expect to be informed of the pros and cons of different approaches and fully consulted when it comes to a choice of continuation or cessation of radical treatment.

Last, many hospices are under pressure to take patients who have AIDS and admission policies have had to be re-examined (Hospice Information Service, unpublished). As far as infection is concerned it seems that the presence of the AIDS virus in an individual should not cause more problems to other patients or staff than the presence of Hepatitis B and that ward procedures must be correct and safe for all. It follows that the acceptance of appropriate patients who happen to be sero-positive or have HIV-induced terminal malignancies is thus likely to be the policy of many hospices. Reservations remain about taking patients with non-malignant manifestations which require vigorous investigations and prophylaxis, as well as treatment, for which hospices have neither the facilities nor the skills.

Other problems connected with admission of AIDS patients are emerging but are not necessarily insurmountable. They include the difference in age groups – hospices can appear very fuddy-duddy places to lively gay groups – and difficulties in caring for demented patients in homely small wards open to gardens, courtyards and other wards. A less tangible problem relates to the way in which the disease has been transmitted. Understandably, because of discrimination suffered by people with AIDS, there is insistence on absolute confidentiality up to, and including the cause of death as stated on the certificate. Cancer also was once a dread word to be whispered or cloaked in euphemism and evasion. The hospice movement set out not to break confidentiality or to force hard and unwelcome facts on patients and families but to give "opportunities to express deeper fears and encouragement to both patients and families to share as much of the truth as can safely be handled" (Saunders & Baines 1983). AIDS-related secrecy might be difficult for hospices to handle.

By no means all of these problems apply when considering home care for patients with AIDS. Hospice teams may develop this as a natural extension of their work in the community in conjunction with existing domiciliary services. But they might be likely, for the time being, to turn to a hospital unit for back-up beds rather than a hospice.

HOSPICE – THE PATTERN OF PROVISION

If the patients cared for within hospices are likely to continue to be predominantly those with symptoms of terminal cancer what of the pattern of care and the envelope in which it is delivered?

The explosion of hospice development in the independent sector has given rise to concern (Hillier 1985). Some have run into severe financial problems, others have owed more to an attitude of "what others have, we must have" than to the response of a community to real needs. Problems of standards may arise when units are isolated from mainstream clinical practice. This was seen in the past when a few long-stay NHS hospitals for elderly or mentally ill people failed to keep up with the developments and good practice to be found in other specialist units and general hospitals. One or two of the specialist cancer charities promote conferences and workshops with the objective of maintaining standards and encouraging the spread of good ideas. The danger that the term "hospice" itself might be thought to confer a guarantee of good care must be recognised.

From 297 beds in 58 in-patient units and 32 home care teams and eight hospital support teams in Britain in 1980 (Lunt & Hillier 1981) there are now 2161 beds in 117 units with nearly a 100 home care teams and 20 hospital support teams. Another 40 hospice projects (not all inpatient units) are in the pipeline (Hospice Information Service 1987).

Given the precarious financing of many hospices and teams and the comparatively small scope for diversification can this scale of development continue? The crystal ball here becomes murky with both favourable and unfavourable considerations. The green light for further development is the professional, public and political support for this work. This is demonstrated by a 1987 government circular to health authorities requiring the review of the provision of facilities "for dying patients whatever their diagnosis and to plan to rectify deficiencies, where possible in collaboration with the voluntary sector" (DHSS 1987). The red light includes the struggle for revenue funding, problems over standards and the lack of training schemes for medical staff wishing to concentrate on this aspect of care.

It could be argued that a really successful hospice movement would do itself out of a job and that the principles of symptom control, treating the whole person and supporting the family, would be absorbed by the community and in general hospitals. To some extent this is happening and making in-patient beds in separate units far less necessary. Home care teams and hospital support teams function in an advisory capacity, without taking over full responsibility, bridging gaps between patients in their homes and those looking after them there and in hospitals. Such arrangements enable general practitioners and hospital staff to continue looking after their patients until the end even if they have had little experience of this work. Increasing emphasis on the care of the dying patient and his family in medical and nursing curricula (pre- and postgraduate) is having a number of effects: it raises the level of awareness of what can be done; imparts information on a theoretical and practical level; and points people toward centres of expertise which can advise on particularly difficult cases.

However, pressures in large general wards within acute hospitals may be hard to overcome while care at home may cease to be possible for a number of reasons, both clinical and social. The extent to which teams working with patients in their own homes need to be able to admit patients to an in-patient facility quickly in an emergency, or to prevent breakdown of the family, is variable. Many staff operating in the community would regard lack of such arrangements as detrimental to the services they provide. A universally applied policy of basing terminal care services on teams operating without beds would have the added drawback that such arrangements provide inadequate experience or training for individuals still on the learning curve and research on symptom control would be much more difficult to pursue.

Volunteers play a particularly important part in hospice work and are used in a variety of ways from ward duties or sorting through goods for hospice shops, to transporting or helping patients in their own homes. Supporting carers or more extensive involvement with looking after patients in their own homes is a likely extension and may perhaps be further stimulated by what is happening in the AIDS field. But the role of volunteers which is developing significantly is that of bereavement counselling. Elisabeth Earnshaw-Smith and Paddy Yorkstone (1986) have described setting up and running a bereavement service and include detailed advice on selection and training of people for this "channel through which an understanding of loss and bereavement can be conveyed, and ideas about ways of helping can be spread to ordinary people".

Regional variations in the mix and match between in-patient units, symptom control teams and nursing teams in the community seem likely to continue. The bigger units are already playing an important part in training staff – both those who intend a career in this field and those who wish to have this training because of its relevance to their work in another specialty. It would be desirable to have at least one such unit with 25 beds or more in each region, preferably close (geographically and in other ways) to a general hospital, possibly a teaching hospital.

The specialties and facilities of the hospital, such as radiotherapy, oncology, neurosurgery, and a pain clinic, as well as the full gamut of district specialties, would emphasize the multi-specialty aspects of terminal care. The great value of swift surgery or radiotherapy for some patients where the spinal cord is compressed and the contribution of nerve blocks and epidural analgesia in a small but important proportion would be demonstrable. Such arrangements would also provide excellent opportunities for more precise studies such as appraising the value of chemotherapy in late stage malignant disease or evaluating the role of antidepressants in treating severe and chronic pain. A unit thus situated would also have a home care team and day centre together with educational facilities which would be used by all the caring disciplines including social workers and hospital chaplains. It would provide training at a senior level for medical and nursing staff using the facilities of the unit. In addition staff from the unit would take part in teaching activities and rounds on the main site as their expertise on symptom control and breaking bad news comes to be valued by staff in other specialties. Some units are already developing such programmes and places on courses are much in demand as the number of career posts for medical and nursing staff increases.

Other districts might have similarly dedicated but smaller units within the district general hospital or in its grounds together with a variety of Macmillan teams and arrangements with hospices including Sue Ryder Homes and Marie Curie Memorial Foundation Homes, and community nurses working from them. The liaison function between these disparate bodies is already important and likely to become more so. Care of the dying is not enhanced by squabbles over geographical boundaries or the location of ultimate responsibility. A speedy response to requests for help is essential. Links with social services are also important as provision of home care may depend on a variety of support such as home helps, incontinence services and night sitters as well as the strictly professional. Cancer is predominantly a disease of the elderly and in the small families of our day by no means everybody has any carer who can take responsibility – let alone a network of close family members prepared to support the principal carer.

HOSPICE – THE CONTENT OF CARE

This chapter has so far looked at the patients likely to be cared for within hospices and the question whether the nature and content of the care that patients receive will change is much more difficult to address. In the 20 years of its existence St Christopher's Hospice has seen a shortening of length of stay, an increase in very ill patients referred for the last few days of life, and an increase in the number of patients the St Christopher's home care team looks after in conjunction with general practitioner and domiciliary services. Some of this may be due to changes in modes of giving ordinary analgesic agents which have been more striking and more useful than any changes in the substances contained in the pharmocopoeia. Slow release morphine has removed the need for a four hourly regimen in many cases. The syringe driver, which automatically delivers measured amounts of analgesic, antiemetic or other substances, avoids the need for repeated injections in those who can no longer take medication orally and enables some patients to remain at home who otherwise would require admission or very frequent visits from the domiciliary nursing service. The development of epidural modes of delivery, including implantable reservoirs, has greatly improved the prospects of pain control in the very small proportion of individuals who appear to be resistant to oral morphine or where the side effects from oral administration are not tolerated (Cherry & Gourlay 1987). Research on the substances which exist in the brain and spinal cord and which act as transmitters of stimuli – including pain – is likely to identify other ways of coping in those rare instances where patients have very severe pain which does not respond to the analgesics in common use now. Other avenues ripe for study are the measurement of pain and the evaluation of symptom control – never easy subjects involving as they do so much that can vary between observers of different disciplines.

Increasingly units are establishing a full mix of different professions including a chaplain as well as medical, nursing and social work staff and a variable number of therapists usually physio sometimes occupational or diversional. This multi-disciplinary approach is bound to continue as the quality of care is greatly enhanced when each discipline understands and appreciates the contribution of others. Training programmes for medical staff intending a lifetime career in this work are developing as it is increasingly recognised that supervision from a distance by a consultant or general practitioner with other duties may not be very satisfactory save as an interim measure.

One difference between the American and British scene is the comparative rarity here of psychiatrists with training or experience – or perhaps interest – in this work. A few very well-known individuals prevent there being a complete dearth but more medical staff with psychiatric training would be very welcome. The distinction between sadness and depression in patients near the end of their days is not easy to make and staff need help to do this particularly those in support teams whose contacts with patients may be quite brief. This is not to say that every patient must be seen by a psychiatrist but to emphasise that training in care of dying patients should include the recognition of treatable psychiatric conditions. Similarly staff need to know which family member or friend is most at risk of breakdown in the near future or of long-term psychiatric morbidity if both these are to be avoided.

Inevitably staff working in this field have to develop skills of listening and communicating and there is a growth in interest in this within many training establishments. Hospice staff are often asked to talk about communication, perhaps under the heading of "Breaking bad news". Significant advances can be claimed (not necessarily attributable to hospices or their staff) in this field. Techniques such as role play and exposure via video tapes (Buckman & Maguire) or multi-disciplinary courses are increasingly being used wherever care of patients is being taught and can, surely, do nothing but good for staff and patients alike.

The needs of people with AIDS and patients with AIDS, together with their families and friends, for support and counselling has focussed attention on the work with families which has already been established in association with hospices. Bereavement counselling already has an extensive literature and, of course, is not confined to relatives or friends of patients with any particular diagnosis. The stresses and strains of all those, professional or not, working with the dying from whatever cause are being explored and may lead to prevention of burn out or battle fatigue in staff as well as serious psychiatric problems in the bereaved. For staff perhaps it will not be formal mechanisms such as support groups but careful selection, appropriate training and recognition that individuals need to identify and nurture their own sources of support. For families and friends the staff themselves are a means of strength. Their involvement with the dying person and the respect they pay to that person helps families and friends to cope through sharing the bewilderment and pain of loss.

A feature of hospice philosophy from the start has been the extent to which it has been moulded and influenced by patients themselves. As Saunders and Baines (1983) state: "We may be working with long and sometimes distressing physical retreats but these are so often more than balanced by emotional and spiritual advances. It is not to idealize to say that achievements are constantly being made during this time. From the dying themselves we learn not only to understand something of the ending of life but also a great deal to make us optimistic about all life and about the potential of those ordinary human beings who work their way through it."

CONCLUSION

It is tempting to say that in the future hospices will continue to do what they do now – but rather better. The great growth in literature on care of the dying is evidence of the intense study to which it is being subjected (Greenall). Principles and methods of symptom control will continue to be taught both to those caring for the dying and those in related specialties where this approach is relevant. New generations of staff from all disciplines will look critically at what is being done and what is being taught and care of patients in home, hospital or hospice will continue to improve as knowledge and expectations both increase.

Counselling and work with families and friends will continue to develop and hospices will be a focus for this. Teaching and training of specialists and of those who are working in different but related fields is likely to expand if present demand is an indication. A proper research base, within the bigger units, is needed for sound teaching and maintenance of standards throughout hospice work.

The development of specialist services for dying patients and their families might be thought to be a takeover by the professionals. From within the hospice the feeling is exactly opposite. The realisation that the courage and commonsense of patients and their families can triumph in crisis has caused professionals to see their own roles not only as prescriptive but also as enabling and supporting. Alleviating symptoms enables patients to continue to be people rather than vehicles of distress; people who, in spite of their dependence, can continue to exercise choice and control over the nature and place of treatment and care.

Saunders, C M "The challenge of terminal care" in *Scientific Foundation of Oncology*. Edited by Symington, T & Carter, R L. Heinemann Medical Books. 1976.

Hospice Information Service. St Christopher's Hospice. May 1987.

"Hospice comes of age". *Lancet* (editorial) 3 May 1986.

Ford, G R "Training for work in hospices" (correspondence column) *Lancet* 17 May 1986.

Hospice Information Service. St Christopher's Hospice. Unpublished survey.

Saunders, C M & Baines, M J. *Living with dying: The Management of Terminal Disease*. Oxford University Press. 1983.

Hillier, R "Hospice UK – 2000 AD". *Journal of Palliative Care* 1 (1) 9–15 September 1985.

Lunt, B & Hillier, R "Terminal care: present services and future priorities". *British Medical Journal* 29 August 1981.

Hospice Information Service. St Christopher's Hospice. May 1987.

DHSS *Health Services Development: Terminal Care* HC (87) 4.

Earnshaw-Smith, E & Yorkstone, P *Setting up and Running a Bereavement Service*. St Christopher's Hospice. 1986.

Cherry, D A & Gourlay, G K "The spinal administration of opioids in the treatment of acute and chronic pain". *Palliative Medicine* 1 (2) 89–106 June 1987.

Buckman, R & Maguire, P *Why won't they talk to me?* (Series of 5 videotapes). Linkward Productions Ltd Middlesex.

Greenall, B L *The Development of the UK Hospice Movement 1976–81 as Reflected in the Growth of Relevant Literature*. Polytechnic of North London. 1982.

7

Stillbirth, miscarriage and termination

Lesley Reilly

To facilitate healthy grieving, it needs first to be acknowledged that a loss has taken place. In the case of stillbirth, miscarriage or therapeutic termination, the object of that loss is a child. In practice birth and death are confused when it happens at one and the same time, one cancelling out the other. It is interesting that registration of the stillborn child reinforces that attitude.

Culturally we are not encouraged to grieve. It is important for the carer to recognise that parents who lose a child before it is born have similar mourning needs as if the child had been born alive.

It is important when working with couples who have lost a baby to help them to build an identity for the infant. Until recent years babies born dead were simply taken away and disposed of, the parents not seeing the infant and not being encouraged to say goodbye, in the accepted ritualistic way, with a funeral. This can have profound implications. A mother sought my help to find where her baby, stillborn 12 years ago, was buried. For 12 years the location of her baby had been a significant unresolved issue, even though she has three other healthy children.

It is necessary to preface the remainder of this chapter by attempting some definitions. There seems to be unanimous agreement that a baby born dead after 28 weeks gestation is regarded as a stillbirth. However, there seems to be some confusion about what a miscarriage is and more confusion, with possible drastic consequences, about what abortion is. Abortion is the technical name for the baby lost before 28 weeks gestation. What for the professionals is an abortion, for the layperson is a miscarriage. Abortion to the layperson suggests a deliberate, and until recent years, a criminal act of voluntarily ending a pregnancy.

Modern technology is developing to such a degree that babies are surviving at 23 weeks gestation. Whatever the ethical implications, it does mean that the cut-off point of 28 weeks for defining a miscarriage or stillbirth is being increasingly recognised as being outmoded and hopefully with time the definition of 28 weeks as the cut-off point will be speedily reviewed.

It is also clear from the above definition, that there is an urgent need to examine the word "abortion". Doctors may argue that this is purely a technical term, but so was "imbecile", in its day. There is a strong argument for adopting a more acceptable term. Redefining the language we use helps to redefine our attitudes. Imagine the mother losing her baby at 26 weeks and hearing it being described as an abortion.

Possibly, the internationally agreed and recommended definition by the World Health Organisation in 1950 may be more acceptable, but this has yet to be established by the professions. This was that "fetal death" described death, at *any* stage in pregnancy, before delivery. This was further defined as early fetal death for loss up to 19 weeks gestation, intermediate fetal death for a loss between 20 and 28 weeks, and late fetal death after 28 weeks.

Background

It is probable that as many as 75 per cent of all conceptions are miscarried before pregnancy is suspected and confirmed. That staggering figure perhaps gives a new perspective to the dilemma of miscarriage and the loss of a child. However, what we clearly need to remember to maintain some sense of balance is that these early miscarriages are in the main not known at a conscious level. Therefore no attachment has been made and the loss has no impact on the individual.

For every 100 confirmed pregnancies, between 15 and 20 babies are delivered before 28 weeks. For every 100 confirmed pregnancies, one of these pregnancies will end in a stillbirth. Of those, 35 per cent show no pathology at post-mortem, perhaps dispelling some of the myths that doctors have all the answers.

The probable course of events when a mother miscarries, at any stage in her pregnancy, will depend on a number of factors: which of her local consultants is to look after her; what the bed state is in her local hospital; what the individual carer's particular attitude is to a patient who is losing her baby. It is difficult to identify when, during the gestational period, a mother about to lose her unborn child ceases to be a medical problem with an unfortunate outcome and becomes a mother about to lose her child.

Until recent years mothers coming to hospital because their pregnancy was ending, would be dealt with on the gynaecology ward up to 28 weeks and then the maternity ward if the gestation period was more than 28 weeks. However, because babies are now surviving before 28 weeks, a mother losing her baby after between 20 and 22 weeks gestation, is likely to be dealt with on the maternity ward. This has emotional and practical implications. At an emotional level, since the woman is treated as a sick person, she is treated as a patient not as a mother about to lose her baby. This clearly is the beginning of the end of her identity as a mother and consequently the identity of the lost object, the baby. The infant is likely to be disposed of in some way unknown to the mother and this is likely to conjure up images of her baby being abandoned, incinerated, disposed of. It is not likely that there will be any follow-up in the community if a woman is dealt with on the gynaecology ward. There is no community midwife to validate the woman's identity as a mother. Some health visitors, perhaps out of a sense of caring, tend not to do follow up visits, wary of distressing their patients.

Further, if a mother is dealt with on the gynaecology ward, after the event, there is a medical procedure to "clean-up" anything left in the womb and she is discharged home as quickly as possible. The agonies of childbirth the mother has gone through are the equivalent of an attack of appendicitis when there is nothing at the end of it, not even a dead baby.

The diagnosis of the still-born child may happen before the onset of labour and the implications of having a dead baby in her womb will mean different things to different women. Some mothers will react by wanting the baby to be taken away immediately, not being able to see herself as anything but a "walking coffin", that what she is carrying is somehow dirty, rotting inside her. Other mothers need time to accept that their baby is dead, hoping that perhaps the doctors are wrong in their diagnosis, that as the baby was given life in her womb originally, perhaps if she retains the infant she can do it again. It is true to say that doctors are reluctant to induce a dead baby because of the possibilities of various medical complications. It is easy to imagine a baby rotting inside, but in fact, the contents of the womb remain sterile for some time. It is possible that the mother will go into spontaneous labour, her body rejecting naturally the lifeless contents of her womb and therefore it is believed advisable that an induction should not be carried out immediately the diagnosis is made.

In the past the still-born infant would be whisked away and parents advised not to see their baby and maybe considered morbid if they wanted to see a photograph of their child. Attitudes have changed. With hindsight it seems incomprehensible that the parents of a dead baby should be advised not to see their child. But if we take that further what seems equally difficult to understand is that today we ask parents if they want to see their dead baby. Perhaps what would be more normal would be to assume the parents want to be with their baby unless they say otherwise. Culturally this is alien to us but for a successful mourning experience, seeing and holding the baby gives it an identity and the parents valuable memories and they have substance to mourn.

After delivery it is likely that mother will be on a post-natal ward but probably in a single room away from the other mothers and babies. This is likely to happen because staff want to be sensitive to her needs and to protect her from the emotional experience of seeing other mothers and babies. In many cases this is probably true, but one of the consequences of separation of the mother who has lost her baby can be feelings of isolation, feeling unclean and loneliness. It may be a little early to face other mothers and babies but this will have to be done at some stage. It could be considered more valuable if the trauma is faced in the safety of the maternity unit, surrounded by carers and mothers who perhaps themselves have lost a baby, than being alone in the high street seeing a baby in a pram and having no shelter, either physical or emotional. What appeared to be an easy decision has deeper implications, of which professionals and lay people need to be aware.

The decision to discharge early to help the mother "get back to normal" could again have the opposite effect. Studies by Lovell (1983) and Horowitz (1978) show that families are not comfortable dealing with the loss of a pregnancy and allow little space for the mother to talk. Fathers are expected to be the strong ones and are allowed even less space to talk, while mothers who have lost babies are reluctant to talk to family members because they fear that they will be seen as neurotic and think they should quickly get over a still-birth.

One common misunderstanding held by parents in still-birth is that they will not be allowed to bury their baby. In fact to bury a baby born after 28 weeks gestation, the procedure is exactly the same as for an adult. For a baby before 28 weeks gestation, when the registrar is not involved, the undertaker simply needs a letter from a doctor to say that the remains to be buried are, in fact, human remains.

Grief

Grief is what we feel following a loss, mourning is the process of coming to terms with the loss, and if this is frustrated we remain vulnerable for the rest of our lives.

Grief for a lost baby creates the same feelings as with anyone to whom we have been attached. Numbness, denial, anger, depression, longing; the list is familiar. The tasks we perform during the mourning process are equally painful but necessary. Acknowledging the loss to oneself and to the outside world, talking about the lost person to give him substance, disposing of possessions, in this case the layette; the tasks continue. It is clear that parents of a lost baby go through the same process.

It is a very difficult and, indeed, skilled task to recognise and assess inappropriate responses to grief. We all, as individuals, bring to the process of mourning, our life's experiences, our particular relationship with the lost object and our relationship to our external world. What is proper mourning for one individual may be maladaptive for another. The casual, loose and negative use of the word "morbid" in our society does not take into account the individuality of the potential mourning response. We should not be so quick to describe something as "morbid" for we may be condemning our clients and creating further guilt for a response that is totally appropriate for them.

There is a profound difference in the grief process when mourning a child that never lived outside the mother's womb, the lack of the identity of the child and invariably the cutting short of the rights of passage afforded other human beings. Not having a funeral can interfere with the climate of accepting the task to be achieved before an individual can move on from grief to reinvest in the future.

When grieving for the loss of someone who has lived, we have mementoes, anniversaries and memories. When grieving for a child lost before birth we have nothing but dashed hopes, aspirations and opportunities.

To allow more open grieving, it is imperative that the child's identity be established and made firm in reality and in the mind. This can be done in different ways to suit the parents concerned, as well as naming the child and having photographs. A footprint will also act to give memories substance. Cot cards, wrist bands and certificates all form part of the permanent memories for the parents. In addition, if they feel able to, or want to do so, parents may wish to write down their account of the event and their feelings. This, as well as being a memento, would also act as a tool for understanding their reactions and ultimately accepting their loss. Building the child's identity also serves to maintain and strengthen the woman's identity, when she may feel she has failed as a woman and as a mother.

Some modern maternity units, including my own, have a room and all the attendant facilities to allow parents and close family to be with their baby for as long as they wish, to have time to make decisions that have in the past been made hurriedly and later regretted, for example, plans for the funeral.

People caring for bereaved parents – friends, family and professionals – will have different relationships with the couple and will have differing skills to offer. But perhaps the most common skills which each can bring into play are to listen and allow emotion to be shown without discomfort. It is wise to remember that if a person cries in a state of mourning, it is not because damage has been done by the person who is talking to them, but it is the grief being expressed and anyone helping the patient, client, or friend, through bereavement, should see distress as a positive sign and not try to avoid it. We do not distress the bereaved, they are sharing their distress and loss with us.

Professionals have an inherent worry that if they show the human side of themselves to a client by, for example, crying with him, then they somehow lose their professional identity. But the opposite is true: the professional is seen to have the added quality of also being human. The only time this type of response becomes a problem is when it interferes with the competence of the professional.

Termination

In the case of voluntary loss of pregnancy, reactions are ambivalent: on the one hand anxiety and guilt, on the other relief. In the case of a termination for social reasons it is the ending of an unwanted pregnancy. In the case of the therapeutic termination, it is the reassurance achieved when, after delivery, the parents can see for themselves the problems their baby had and be reassured that they had made the right decision.

Women who undergo a termination, whether for medical or social reasons, may suffer a similar grief reaction to those women whose pregnancy ends involuntarily. It is possible that the guilt reaction could be more marked but considerable research (Payne *et al.* 1976; Pariser *et al.* 1978; Drower & Nash 1978) seems to indicate that while the grief process can be the same for women who seek termination, it is likely to resolve itself much more quickly as the outcome was actively sought. Only when women enter into the termination process without appropriate preparation are psychological problems likely to result.

Death is a part of life, grief is a way of celebrating life in recognising death. It is a painful road which individuals will travel at different speeds and in different vehicles depending on their experiences of life, but what is important to remember when caring for parents who lose a baby is that they have a need to talk and to have someone listen and in doing so give their grief credibility. They need to be listened to, for the only reassurance they require is to know that their feelings are normal. The helper should help and be careful not to judge.

Parents need create as much of an identity as possible for their child and handling whatever they have – their memories, photographs and so on – is important. Only when the baby's identity has been fully constructed can parents finally let him go.

The social worker can be the vital link when a pregnancy is going to be lost, not only in helping parents begin to work through the mourning period successfully, but to help other professionals and the family deal with their feelings and, thereby, help the parents deal with theirs.

British Association of Social Workers *Termination of the Abnormal Fetus and Stillbirth*. Special Interest Group. 1986.

Broome, A "Termination of pregnancy" in *Psychology and Gynaecology Problems*. Tavistock. 1984.

Drower, S J & Nash, E S "Therapeutic abortion on psychiatric grounds: Part 11, The continuing debate". *South African Medical Journal* 16: 643–7. 1978.

Harvey, P "You are saying goodbye to someone you never said hello to". *Community Care*. 24 November 1983.

Horowitz, N "Adolescent mourning, reactions to infant and fetal loss". *Social Casework*, pp 551–8. 1978.

Lovell, A "Women's reactions to late miscarriage, stillbirth and perinatal death". *Health Visitor*. September 1983.

Lovell, A "Some questions of identity, late miscarriage, stillbirth and perinatal loss". Vol. 17, pp 755–61. *Social Science & Medicine*. 1983.

Pariser, S F, Dixon, K N & Thatcher, K M "The psychiatric abortion consultation". *Journal of Reproductive Medicine*. 21 (31): 171–6. 1978.

Payne, E C, Kravitz, A R, Notman, M J & Anderson, J "Outcome following therapeutic abortion". *Archives of General Psychiatry*. 33: 725–33. 1976.

Potts, M, Diggory, P & Peel, J *Abortion*. Cambridge University Press. 1977.

8

Death in residence

Chris Hanvey

"Someone's moved in. Someone's taken poor Mary Morgan's place. Her chair and her bed. Like a ruddy conveyor belt. They move someone else in before the bed's cold."

Sadly, the formidable Mrs Jessop, in Lance Salway's novel (1979) is reflecting a popular view of residential care. Death is simply the final stage on a conveyor belt between independence and the grave; to be cursorily dealt with, practically accommodated and summarily dismissed. A major advantage for staff is that it frees a bed and allows the whole process to start again.

This chapter is about the way death and bereavement in residential care can and should be dealt with. It is based on a national survey and attempts to keep both feet firmly placed in everyday practice. While making reference to what might necessarily be regarded as "bad" procedures, more importantly it tries to look at the good and indicate pointers to methods of responding to death and bereavement in ways that are both sensitive and sympathetic. It is written against a background of ambiguous societal attitudes to death, where education for death or "thanatology", as it is known in America, rarely figures on public curricula. It is also written with an awareness that death in residential settings affects not only the dying person but families and those charged with the privilege of caring. Lastly it has been written with the implicit assumption that caring for those who are dying will remind us of our own frailty and mortality and that the stages of mourning characterised by such authors as Dr Elizabeth Kübler Ross as "denial", "anger", "bargaining", "depression" and "acceptance" (1970) may be as much the response of staff as of those whose deaths are imminent.

It also needs to be acknowledged that, since we are considering death in residential care, the main, but not exclusive, focus will be elderly people. About two-thirds of deaths in Great Britain took place either in hospitals or residential homes and, statistically, the chances are that a resident in a home for elderly people will witness and be affected by up to ten deaths every year. A survey of 175 homes for elderly people, conducted by Booth *et al.*, not unnaturally discovered that mortality rose progressively with age (1983). So 15 per cent of their sample of 699 residents died under 80 years old, 23 per cent were berween 80 and 89 and 34 per cent were 90 and over. The study also revealed that the length of time in care was an important factor. The first few months in residential care appear to be a period of considerable vulnerability and there may be some correlation between the immediate loss of independence and the will to live. Statistically, then, old people's homes, like hospitals, can be seen as very dangerous places in which to live!

To gain additional material for this chapter, a letter was widely circulated, both generally to magazines concerned with social work and more specifically to those journals aimed at the care of elderly people. The letter asked for experiences in working with death and bereavement in residential care and gave an assurance that any follow-up by the author would be treated in the strictest confidence. A total of 47 replies were received, with over 60 per cent coming from people working directly in residential care. These included hospices, hospitals, hostels for mentally handicapped and mentally ill people, old people's homes and an intermediate treatment centre. Surprisingly, at the time, the letter appeared to open the floodgates into powerful, and one suspected, previously unspoken feelings. Individual reminiscences told of the unfeeling way that some deaths had been accepted, the first unannounced discovery of a death and misguided attempts to pretend to other residents that indeed no death had occurred. Correspondents spoke further of coffins smuggled through back entrances, bodies disappearing in plastic bin liners and a studious avoidance of death, "as it was thought to be rather depressing"*. For it was, as one letter recorded "far easier to deal with the practical tasks around death and to avoid the feelings".

Many respondents pointed to two initial problems, particularly in caring for elderly people. First, the assumption that elderly people always wanted to live and second, the difficulty of not simply taking "any death just as a matter of course". Clearly, there must be a considered distinction here between sudden and predicted death, but for those who have the privilege of preparation, it was often essential that this was done in a relaxed and contemplative fashion. As Sarton (1983) writes: "I want to be ready, to have gathered everything together and sorted it out as if I were preparing for a great journey".

Indeed, problems can come when we refuse to accept the preparation for death as a major purpose of an old persons' home and therefore often render the occupants mute. Furthermore, as one respondent challengingly asked, perhaps there is no place for short-term care in a home which is involving residents and staff in a life together that ends in death, rather than in a return home.

Many respondents stressed the need to ensure that, primarily,

* All quotations, unless otherwise stated, are taken from respondents who took part in the survey.

the medical requirements of those dying in residential care were protected. It is worth noting, in parenthesis, that with the development of social work education and CCS or CQSW trained staff, it is perhaps less likely than previously that nursing backgrounds amongst senior staff can be assumed.

The first responsibility is to relieve the pain, provide medication and ensure that medical help is always available. Balanced diets to avoid or relieve constipation should be provided; those still reasonably mobile should be encouraged to sit in a chair or up in bed supported by pillows and those who are bed-bound should be encouraged to lie on their sides and should be changed from side to side every two hours. Pressure sores, particularly in areas affected by sweat, urine or faeces can be relieved by keeping skin dry and clean, together with bed linen free from wrinkles and crumbs. If catheters have been inserted, then surrounding skin should be creamed and pressure relieved. Lastly it is often important for elderly people to retain relationships with family doctors that have become tried and tested over the years. They require both faith in the medical care they are offered and, when necessary, simple non-technical explanations that help illness and its treatment to be readily understood.

But if preparation for death is important to residents, it is equally vital that staff, too, are ready. Many homes keep a section of the file in which essential information is carefully recorded: next of kin, details of where wills are to be found, requests regarding burial or cremation and inventories of personal possessions. Often people who are admitted to old people's homes have, themselves, been recently bereaved and this, when sensitively handled, may assist them in acknowledging the necessity to "sort things out". Such preparation should extend to families and relatives, effecting reconciliations when this is possible, encouraging family visits and creating an atmosphere where past, present and future can be honestly acknowledged.

Few areas of social work practice could involve more skills than the work necessary during death itself. As one respondent sensitively recorded: "You inherit years of previous behaviour in dealing with death."

There can be no easy answers to questions such as how much information should be given. "Mankind", as T S Eliot asserted, "cannot bear too much reality", and people vary in the reality they can bear. But the hospice movement has taught us, both to give control back to the dying and to encourage an open atmosphere, free from deception and permitting, where possible, the simplest and most truthful statements about prognosis. Often such deceptions can be almost farcically mutual, with both staff and dying people aware that death is imminent but not able to face each other with the truth. Usually, when this deception can be overcome and death acknowledged, relationships can also be deepened and the serious work of "letting go" begin. While most old people do not wish to be left alone while dying, there often comes a time, as several respondents noted, when it becomes necessary to let go and the dying person may wish to be alone. Dying children are sometimes better at understanding and dealing with this than more fearful adults and it may involve very skilled staff to recognise the needs of the dying person and, when necessary, suggest the withdrawal of friends or relatives.

Sometimes such nursing care cannot be done within the home itself and a transfer to hospital becomes necessary. Most respondents spoke of the considerable efforts that were often gone through to avoid such a move, involving a level of nursing care and commitment that went beyond mere job descriptions. When such a move is necessary, the visits of other relatives, residents and staff are particularly important and whenever possible it is essential to retain beds for a hoped-for return.

Few aspects of death in residential care evoked more bitter comments from respondents than the removal of bodies once death had occurred. One person wrote: "The removal of a body would take place when residents were not about." And another said: "The county council in their wisdom had economised in the size of the lift – which would not take a coffin. We once carried someone down stairs in a contrivance shaped like a cricket bag." A third stated: "During the time it is made sure that nobody comes out of the unit."

But against these views, might be placed the home where staff had struggled to make the whole process more meaningful and less deceptive: "We have learned to discourage the practice of quick 'back door' removals. Undertakers who insist upon this practice are not called upon again." And: "We very much involve our residents. When the body is being taken to its place of rest the residents all watch and say a prayer for them."

Such procedures appear to be a touchstone against which other aspects of care are frequently judged.

Death itself creates a mix of bureaucratic, practical and emotional requirements. The death must be registered and a coroner informed if, amongst other circumstances, no doctor has attended the deceased in his last illness; the doctor attending the patient did not see him within 14 days before death; death was sudden, unexplained or in suspicious circumstances; death may have been due to an accident, violence or neglect; or death was due to a medical mishap or to drugs or alcohol.

Should cremation have been requested, then an independent medical report will also be required and a cremation form will need to be filled in and given to the undertaker.

Once death has occurred, there is a considerable challenge to face in meeting the needs of residents, relatives and staff.

Respondents differed in the way that the news of a death was broken within the home itself. Several places said it was only necessary to tell one resident and the word would then be spread very rapidly. A close friend or natural leader might be chosen to inform others. In another nameless establishment, an announcement was actually made on the public address system and appropriate verses read out to the assembled company! Residents may need reassurance that the deceased did not suffer and will inevitably be reminded of their own mortality. Often it is necessary for residents to be given "permission" to grieve in an atmosphere that not only accepts but welcomes the expression of deep feelings. For, as one respondent remarked: "Not letting other residents face the death of one of their number actually impoverishes them."

Staff will need added sensitivity to the words and atmosphere of residents, to be aware of signs of aggression, anger or betrayal that are a normal part of such a process. Equally, as another respondent commented: "You need to celebrate the life – but it is difficult to do."

Most staff experience a feeling of panic at having to break the news of death to relatives. One home developed a practice of making a brief phone call to the nearest relative and asking the person to phone back, when the news had been fully absorbed. Again, preparation should have begun well before; relatives should be encouraged to visit, and tea, sympathy and a quiet room should be available for relatives to cope with the impending loss. Ideally, relatives may have assisted in the caring during illness, as this sometimes helps to relieve guilt and to cement bonds that become even more important when the death has occurred. But, as a respondent noted: "Support is only really possible if you have previously had a good relationship." In this context, it also needs to be recognised that feelings can become misdirected as a result of the pressures of events and strengths of powerful feelings: "You need to understand that sometimes it is necessary for relatives to give vent to their anger and grief by pouring out areas of neglect and failings of the establishment and that it is part of good caring practice to allow them to do this".

Experience had shown several respondents that it is also sometimes necessary to wait before help can be offered to those bereaved. Initially it may be a question of listening or, in some instances, putting relatives in touch with other organisations: for example, the Society of Compassionate Friends (for bereaved parents), the National Association of Widows or CRUSE. Some homes have also produced short booklets, with helpful information about undertakers, florists, the registering of death, advice and self-help groups and so on. Several residential staff also found that the occasion when personal possessions were collected, often after a funeral, could be a fruitful time for staff to help relatives release their grief. In one hospice a letter is sent on the anniversary of the deceased, to nearest relatives, affirming that the memories remain alive. This, in itself, can provoke fresh contact and new opportunities to work through unresolved feelings.

The task of treating death and bereavement openly, of bringing it out of the shadows and of acknowledging hidden fears, lies heaviest upon the shoulders of the head of home. It is she who needs to ask both of herself and of her staff "What do you fear?"; to recognise that death may have different meanings to staff and residents and to acknowledge the tactics that any staff group understandably use in dealing with death. These have been well characterised by Len Davies (1979) as assuming a number of forms. Foremost is the avoidance of death or dying with carers; for example, studiously avoiding asking the residents how they feel. Alternatively, it becomes possible either to pass the buck ("ask the doctor") or to become involved in fantasies that admit the possibility of some miracle cure. Other techniques involved the selected hearing of information, the denial of painful feelings tentatively offered by the dying person, or conscious assumption that the dying may be personally unaware of what is going on. In these circumstances, we are entitled to ask: whom are staff protecting, the residents or themselves?

Again a number of approaches are needed to counteract such responses and the procedure begins well before any bereavement has taken place. Regular supervision of staff, counselling, group therapy and the involvement of outsiders such as consultants, clergy, doctors or relatives may help to open up discussion and provide mutual support. Such help should enable staff both to express their own grief and to allow such experiences as being constructive and not destructive: "No matter who says you should not get emotionally involved you do, you can't look after a client for years without forming some sort of attachment." Training, staff discussion, regular supervision and mutual support will all reduce the taboo of death. Similarly, encouraging an openness amongst staff should also release trust from residents.

If the staff need this support, so too does the head, who carries the greatest burden of responsibility. Most homes, particularly within the local authority system, are part of some wider organisational structure with support and supervision offered from centrally based staff. The quality of this supervision is crucial. External resources may be required when death is imminent, so that additional hours can be provided for staff who sit with the dying. By providing a high level of support to the head, such a model can then be conveyed in turn to those whom she manages.

One underlying assumption of much of the above discussion

will be a sensitivity to both ethnic and religious considerations. Increasingly, with the challenges of a multi-racial society, staff in residential homes will need to be alert to the religious wishes of residents and potential roles of, for example, iman, rabbi or priest. Space forbids an adequate discussion of this important topic, but there is a responsibility on staff to be familiar with specific customs. Respecting religious and ethnic customs is absolutely essential: said one correspondent: "We usually hold a memorial service, as an opportunity to make our farewells – it is also a way of resolving 'unfinished business'". While another wrote: "We usually have a service and sing favourite hymns of the dead person. I also quote the words of Socrates: 'Now it is time we were going, I to die, you to live, but which of us has the happier prospect is unknown to anyone but God.'"

Lastly, two quite special areas of death and bereavement in residential care require reference. The first of these is suicide which, again, deserves a discussion to itself. It poses particular problems, creating anger and guilt both in the staff and in fellow residents: "It's like someone having crept up out of the shadows on one's blind side and suddenly flinging themselves in front of you."

Suicide is frequently perceived as an aggressive act, removing from people their ability to respond to cries for help and leaving them with a sense of total powerlessness. Rarely will staff skills be tested so far and it is essential that feelings are expressed and communications are open enough to permit the total community to understand and grieve together. Respondents who had experienced suicide within their homes, spoke of the corrosive nature of such experiences, eating away at good health when feelings were not given honest expression.

Ainsa (1981) posed four sets of questions which needed to be answered in nursing permanently ill children. Again this subject deserved detailed consideration and equally it will be seen that the questions have a validity for dying adults:

☐ is the child aware of his condition?
☐ if the child does not know, when will he be told?
☐ how do the parents feel and will they object if you converse with the child on the topic of death?
☐ what is the child's physical condition and state of mind?

While death may be quite a usual occurrence in some homes for severely handicapped children, it is rarely part of the everyday experience of residential child care staff. Indeed some of the most poignant letters described deaths that had concerned children. In one instance, a child died after artificial respiration had failed. The police had to be called, to take statements, since treatment had resulted in some bruising on the side of the child's face. "In some instances, work with the staff is almost as important as work with the children," said one member of staff.

This chapter has done little more than raise a few issues and provides an introduction to a complex area of social work practice. Like the response to death itself, it alternates between practical considerations, such as death certificates and funeral arrangements, and the fulfilment of deeper emotional and spiritual needs. There is a level at which any residential home's response to death will provide a yardstick for its health in many other areas of its daily living. Somerset Maughan's caustic advice was that death was a "dull, dreary affair . . . have nothing to do with it." For those whose daily reality it is, the challenge remains to make it an acknowledged and accepted part of life itself.

Ainsa, T "Teaching the terminally ill child". *Education*. Vol. 101 No. 4. 1981.

Bailey, S M "Gentle into that good night". *Care Concern*. May, pp 21–3, 1984.

Booth, T, Philips, D, Barritt, A, Berry, S, Martin, D N and Melotte, C "Patterns of mortality in homes for the elderly". *Age and Ageing* 12, pp 240–44, 1983.

Davies, L "Facing the fact of death". *Social Work Today*. 24 July 1979.

Kübler Ross, E *On Death and Dying*. Tavistock. 1970.

Meacher, M *Taken for a Ride*. Longman. 1972.

Salway, L *Second to the Right and Straight on till Morning*. Macmillan. 1979.

Sarton, M *As We Are Now*. The Women's Press. 1983.

I would like to acknowledge help from the following people who unselfishly gave their time and ideas: P Blanchard, J R Addison, J Axten, S Banks, I Bell, T Booth, S Britcliffe, D Connell, J Connor, R Cowper, K Day, H Ellis, S Ellison, M Fiddes, B Forth, D Frow, J Halifax, C Hawe, M Ingrams, D Kelly, Y Neville, C Newmarch, R Niblett, C Otterburn, J Pardoe, S Price, J Skelton, G Thompson, B E Todd, F Turner, A Williams, M Winstanley, J Yates.

9

The dying child
Mother Frances Dominica

The dying child can never be seen as an isolated individual but as part of a family. In a whole network of relationships with parents, siblings, grandparents, more distant relatives, school friends, neighbours and others, the child will be the focus of strong and differing emotions and responses. For many families the news, or the realisation, that their child will not recover but will die, is followed by such a rapid succession of events, culminating in the child's death, that their response is chiefly that of bewilderment, numbness and denial. There is not time to reason things through, to work out a pattern of coping or even to accept the reality of what is happening. They will be in a state of shock. Conversations will not necessarily register in their minds, explanations may have little meaning and patterns of behaviour may be exaggerated or out of character. The family will often be heavily dependent on the professionals caring for them and will look to them to be calm, in control of the situation, sensitive and caring. However, in this chapter I will focus less on the emergency situation than on the child who is dying more slowly and on the needs of such a child and his family.

The death of a child is an outrage. It violates our assumption that we can put off facing the reality of death, with all its uncomfortable uncertainties, until ripe old age. The response of the onlooker to this tragedy is more often than not to make himself or herself scarce. When the expectations that modern medicine can cure a sick child are dashed, when there is no hope of recovery and it is clear that the disease is gaining ground, then most people feel inadequate in relating to the family concerned. There is a fear of saying the wrong thing, an embarrassment at the prospect of feelings getting out of control, whether the feelings of the child, the family or the observer. The result for the family, and sometimes for the child, is an experience of isolation and loneliness at the very time when they need support, friendship and love most.

For some families whose child is dying the last hope is that the professionals involved in the care of their child will provide a little of the support, friendship and love they look for. For all families, whether they are supported by relatives and friends or not, the attitude and behaviour of professional staff will remain in their memories for the rest of their lives and can have a profound effect on them, for better or for worse, through the long, painful course of their bereavement. The professional who helps most will be the one whose training, skills and experience are resources readily used for the benefit of the family but not used as a shield behind which the professional shelters. At such a time what the family wants most is a fellow human being who is prepared to relate as such, a person who is not afraid to show feelings or to admit that they do not know or understand the reason for such a tragedy. Pretence or deception are never more out of place than they are here. It is also the role of the professional to enable the child to live until he dies, as fully as that individual child is able, and to help the child and family to live each day and hour, experiencing time as depth rather than length. Above all, the true professional will leave the family feeling that *they* are the ones in control, and that no professional should abrogate that right, however much advice, back-up and support she may be offering. If the family is given this assurance and affirmation, and each one is allowed to behave as the person he or she is, then they will often discover a strength and dignity they did not know they possessed. An imbalance can, on the one hand, make them feel they have been taken over because they are "amateurs", and on the other hand may leave them feeling unsupported. They will often feel that they are abnormal in their feelings and behaviour anyway because they don't seem to conform to the expectations of friends, neighbours and even relatives, and a take-over approach by health professionals will only serve to reinforce this belief.

It is vital to remember that although one may have been involved many times in the care of a child dying of a particular disease or in similar circumstances, the child and family are the true experts and the professional has much to learn from them. There is a delicate balance to be achieved in tentatively offering suggestions or advice on the management of some aspect of the situation yet still respecting their way of doing things. There are, of course, rare exceptions to this, such as mental illness or a personality disorder, where a member of the family responds in a way which is inappropriate to the needs of the child.

THE NEEDS OF PARENTS

At the very time when they are most in need of each other's understanding and co-operation, parents, even in a good marriage, will quite probably find themselves reacting in very different ways, often resenting the fact that their partner does not see things their way and act accordingly. Feelings of guilt and of anger are natural and to be expected. In such an outrageous situation it seems that somewhere along the line someone could and should have done something to prevent this child from dying. A parent will lay blame at their own or someone else's door: "We should have noticed the swelling sooner . . . got him to the doctor . . . insisted on a second opinion . . . gone to a different hospital . . . flown him to California before it was too late." Anger may be levelled at spouse, doctor, hospital, God, self or indeed at the child: "How could he do this to me?"

THE NEEDS OF SIBLINGS AND GRANDPARENTS

Siblings of the dying child will often have a raw deal, with everyone's attention focussed on their sick brother or sister. People talk incessantly of the sick one, rarely about them. Talk about the sick one seems often to be in terms of near-sanctity. No one speaks of *them* as saints so it seems to follow that everyone would rather it was the well one who was dying. Conversations between grown-ups are held in hushed tones, partly overheard. The subject is often hastily changed when the well child enters the room. The surviving brother or sister may think that he or she has been the cause of what is happening, sometimes in as direct a way as a remembered outburst in the past – "I hate you! I wish you were dead!" – or they may fear that they, too, will die.

The well sibling needs as much time, understanding and love as anyone has time and opportunity to give. Denied this, the future may hold serious trouble and distress. In the face of such needs we, the professionals, may often feel inadequate and it is important to remember, first, that the way we listen is more important than what we say and, second, that, like everyone else, what this child wants is the security of human warmth and affection. Friends of the child's own age are often those who give the best support and so it is helpful to ensure that there is plenty of opportunity for this. It goes without saying that the brother or sister who is not yet dying, but who suffers with the same disease as the dying child, for example in an inherited condition, has very special needs.

Siblings are not alone in feeling overlooked; grandparents sometimes feel quite alone and unnoticed. Often they will still be young themselves, seeing the parents of the dying child as their children, and powerless to do anything to protect them. Most people do not imagine they will outlive their children, let alone their grandchildren. "If only it could have been me – after all, I've had a full life", is a commonly expressed sentiment.

It is not usually helpful when the professional tries to reason with the reactions and responses of different members of the family of the dying child, still less to try to convince them that they are irrational. Usually, the only helpful thing is to listen, to absorb and to make it clear that nothing said is so shocking or abnormal that the professional will go away and leave them to it. In saying all this, I am assuming that the professional will be sensitive enough to recognise the times when the family does want to be physically alone.

THE NEEDS OF THE DYING CHILD

The people the dying child needs most are the people who have been closest to him in his life, usually his parents or parent, and brothers and sisters. But he may also need a person or people who have not been so closely involved and whose distress is therefore not as acute. Many types of progressive, irreversible disease in children cause intellectual impairment, with varying degrees of awareness and recognition, sometimes with no discernible response to any stimulus whatsoever. The parents of such children will feel very protective towards them and will often be extremely sensitive in observing the attitude and behaviour of others towards their children. The children need all the tender, loving care we can give them; they also deserve to be treated with the dignity which is the right of every human being.

The child whose intelligence has not been impaired by disease will often know, without necessarily having been told, that he is dying. He will have picked up fragments of conversations, observed his parents' grief, found the relevant section in a medical book or noticed the progress and outcome of the same disease in other children. There is, however, a strong instinct in such a child to protect his parents. Knowing how distressed they become when discussing his illness, he may well decide not to talk about it with them, let alone allow them to know he realises he is going to die rather than get better. So the parents are convinced that he does not know. But the child may want to ask questions, make statements or indeed leave requests affecting the well-being of the people he loves most after he himself has died. So, in building up a relationship of mutual trust, professionals may find themselves filling a need in this way. The questions, "Am I going to get better?" "Am I going to die?" "What is it like when you are dead?" do not lend themselves to text-book answers. The response must be different for each child because each child is different, and it must often include the admission that there are some things we do not know or understand. The cardinal rule is not to lie or attempt to deceive the child. To break this rule is to forfeit the child's trust. It is important to listen to what the child is really asking or saying and to respond with simplicity and honesty.

Undergirding all this the professional has the opportunity of communicating a quiet assurance that the child is safe and will be loved and held whatever the future brings. Children will sometimes make specific requests: "Please will you be with my Mum at the funeral?" or "I want my brother to have my battery car". A sick child may refuse pain-killing drugs, and be prepared to

92

suffer unnecessarily, having perceived that a parent is convinced, despite all assurances to the contrary, that these will shorten his life.

In so many ways a dying child becomes old and wise beyond his years and often assumes the role of parent to his own mother and father. Sometimes the child will feel guilty about the way his illness has affected the family. A 10-year-old girl made plans to commit suicide in the belief that her long-drawn out illness was the cause of the breakdown of her parents' marriage.

The child may sometimes need time for himself, and space away from the immediate family. He may need permission to be a child again or to show the depression he normally tries to conceal. In a prolonged illness, he may suffer feelings of anger and frustration and may rebel against what he sees as the over-protective attitude of parents and other adults. "I may have a sick body," said an 11-year-old girl, "but if only people would believe I'm normal like anyone else inside. Why do some people talk to me as if I were stupid or a baby?" This accusation was levelled against professionals of whom she had had long experience.

Dying adolescents have problems of their own. The well adolescent has problems enough and these are immeasurably compounded. Loneliness and great suffering can result from being cut off from the activities of the peer group. Continued attendance at school, however spasmodic, is preferable to having home tuition as far as most young people are concerned, and where possible it is encouraging to the sick boy or girl to be allowed to take part in hobbies or activities, even in the role of onlooker. This can of course be a valued experience for the peer group and an unparelleled source of growth and education.

Sometimes people try to compensate the dying child by swamping him with expensive toys and presents and by arranging a succession of "treats". Another symptom of the same attitude of over-indulgence is to allow the child to behave in a way which is socially unacceptable, removing previously accepted boundaries and expectations of behaviour. This only serves to take more firm ground from under the child's feet in a world which is becoming increasingly shaky and unpredictable for him. The professional can help family and friends to understand that while the occasional present or special treat is good, the child's greatest need is for the love and sense of security they can give him in their own inimitable way.

It is not always bad for the sick child to see his parents' sorrow – indeed if they always appear bright and cheerful as if nothing were wrong, he may question whether they really care or not. It is one more instance of pretence and deception being more harmful than helpful. The use of euphemisms is unwise too. A child who heard dying described as "falling asleep" spent the remaining three years of his life suffering with severe insomnia.

Children usually perceive life after death as heaven. For children brought up in a specifically or non-specifically Christian culture, heaven means being with a loving, gentle Jesus. It is a mixture of angels and parties and sunshine. For a seven-year-old it was a fabulous gymnasium with a huge trampoline – and all his family and best friends there too! This is the hard part: the dying child knows that most of his family and friends will *not* be there because he is going first. "I wish all four of us, Mummy, Daddy, my sister and me, could all die at the same moment 'cos then nobody would be left behind to be sad," said a twelve-year-old.

CONCLUSION

To be alongside a dying child and his family can be both the most demanding and the most rewarding part of the life of a professional. The most demanding, because such an experience tries our own integrity and our whole approach to both life and death; we can of course choose to put up professional barriers, but by so doing we deny both child and family the warmth and security of the human companionship they need so much. The most rewarding, because by being alongside not only do we absorb some of their suffering and grief, but inevitably we also absorb some of the joy they experience in little things; their heightened sensitivity to goodness, truth and beauty; and their ability to enter friendships in a way they may never have done before, the usual barriers of background, race, religion or age having become irrelevant. It is a profound privilege to be there with child and family.

Those of us who have not ourselves experienced the tragedy of the dying and death of our own beloved child can never say to those who do have that experience, "I know how you feel," but we can listen and learn and be thankful for all that they can and do give to us.

10

Bereavement and mentally handicapped people

Maureen Oswin

Mental handicap is an umbrella term covering a wide range of intellectual disabilities. It should not be confused with mental illness. Sometimes a mental handicap is associated with a medically identifiable syndrome (like Down's syndrome) but there may be no apparent reason for a person being mentally handicapped. Known causes include brain damage at birth, illness of the pregnant mother (rubella), the life-style of the pregnant mother (excessive alcohol, smoking, drug addiction). Child abuse, traffic accidents, serious falls, illnesses such as measles, meningitis, or brain tumours, may cause a child of normal intelligence to suffer irreversible brain damage and subsequent mental handicap and severe physical disabilities. Adults of normal intelligence may likewise become mentally handicapped because of illnesses or accidents which damage the brain.

Many mentally handicapped people are physically mobile and can read and write and handle money efficiently. But if they have severe multiple handicaps caused by cerebral palsy (brain damage before or during birth or soon after), they may have poor sight, hearing defects, speech disorders and reduced mobility and will need help with even very simple tasks. Severe physical handicaps may make them dependent on other people to dress, undress and wash them, carry them to the toilet, feed them and hold their cup for them to drink. People with severe multiple handicaps are not necessarily the most intellectually retarded; indeed, they are usually very aware of their situation and very sensitive to the behaviour of other people. Those who have severe speech disabilities may be able to learn a sign language but if they find this too difficult they will rely on basic communication techniques such as eye contact, nods, facial grimaces and expressive sounds.

Some mentally handicapped people have temporary or prolonged behaviour problems. These are frequently caused by lack of appropriate help, other people's attitudes and an inability to communicate, resulting in frustration, anger and despair. Behaviour disorders may have no apparent cause, however, and take the form of over-active destructive behaviour and even, in a small minority of cases, self-mutilation; people described as "autistic" may suffer from these difficult behaviour disorders and their care will pose great problems to their families and the people who try to help them.

Mentally handicapped people may get employment after leaving school, or attend day centres; but many remain at home all day because there is a shortage of day centres or professionals consider them too handicapped to benefit from centre activities.

Many mentally handicapped people are capable of living independently in ordinary houses with one or two friends or a married partner, having support from their local social services department as necessary. Others prefer to live in staffed houses because they need somebody to help them. Even if a person has multiple disabilities, there is no reason why they should not live in an ordinary house; houses can be adapted and staff made available to help according to the person's particular needs. Unfortunately, however, more than 30,000 mentally handicapped people in England and Wales are still living in mental handicap hospitals due to a lack of appropriate community care.

Most parents dread the idea of "putting away" their mentally handicapped sons and daughters into hospital, so they try to look after them at home for as long as possible. This can mean handicapped people aged in their '40s and '50s remaining at home and being cared for by parents in their seventies and eighties. It is not unknown for parents over 70 years old to be still washing, dressing, lifting, bathing and feeding severely handicapped middle-aged sons and daughters, with very little help being provided by local services. Sometimes the handicapped sons and daughters will themselves begin to care for their ageing ailing parents and take responsibility for the household tasks.

The death of a parent will be a massive and terrible blow to the handicapped person, irrespective of the degree of their handicap. It will cause a frightening break-up of their secure (but often isolated), family life-style, and will create changes and problems for which they may be totally unprepared.

Having a mental handicap does not mean that a person is emotionally insensitive. Mentally handicapped people experience the same distressing emotional reactions to bereavement and loss which are felt by people who are not handicapped – tears, sorrow, anger, feelings of fear and panic, disturbed sleep, temporary loss of abilities, disbelief about what has happened.

"I could not believe it" (40 year old mentally handicapped man).

"I was sort of angry for weeks and kept getting into tempers. It was not like me" (Man with Down's syndrome aged 50).

"I shouted out 'no, no, no it's not true' when they told me. But it was true. I still can't believe it though" (A cerebral palsied woman aged 42).

"I fainted when I was told . . ." (Woman with Down's syndrome aged 29).

"I thought, that is that, she won't suffer anymore" (Mentally handicapped man aged 46).

All bereaved people are vulnerable, but bereaved mentally handicapped people are particularly so because they are at risk of suffering a variety of *additional* distressing experiences caused by other people not recognising or appreciating their needs. Some of their problems are illustrated in the following two stories (here disguised to respect privacy).

Eva was very severely mentally handicapped. Her parents had always had to wash, dress, bath and feed her. She had never been away from home, and did not attend a day centre. For years she had lived a very quiet life in the downstairs front room of her parents' house. As her parents became older and Eva heavier to lift, the little family rarely left their house. Her father died when Eva was 40 years old and her widowed mother continued caring for her alone. When Eva was 45 her mother died.

A few hours after her mother's death Eva was admitted to a long-stay hospital, where within a few weeks she became very withdrawn and the staff had difficulty in getting her to eat. The nurses became very worried about Eva's deteriorating condition and recognised that she was "pining" with grief. At a ward meeting they agreed that Eva ought to have one person assigned to her, to give the personal attention she had received at home, but they were not sure whether this would really help, because even if the shortages of hospital staff allowed for personal assignment nobody could replace Eva's mother with regard to personal affection. The nurses did their best, however, and in the following months Eva was allocated two members of staff: one of the permanent ward staff (a nursing assistant who had been widowed a year before and felt a personal empathy towards Eva's plight), and a student nurse who was particularly interested in multiply handicapped people. The ward sister also found a regular voluntary visitor. She gradually began to eat again and to smile, but it was nearly two years before she regained her former cheerfulness and response to people.

Conclusions: Eva might have suffered less after her mother's death if (a) she had had previous experience of being away from home while her parents had been alive and able to support her through the experience of making new relationships; (b) she had not been moved into residential care immediately after her mother died but had had somebody to stay with her in her own home for a few weeks (perhaps a student nurse, social worker or volunteer); and (c) the hospital staff had had a plan of action ready for the admission of a bereaved person, such as the immediate assignment of staff to give special attention.

Joe was aged 42, and had always lived at home. His elderly mother had been widowed for more than 30 years and Joe was used to being "the man of the house", having responsibility for the garden, locking up at night and winding the clocks. He attended a day centre and had many friends in the neighbour-hood. He had never been to a hostel or considered moving into an ordinary house with any friends because his mother thought he should always live at home. When his mother died Joe was found a temporary place in a hostel, many miles away from his home, so that in addition to his grief at losing his mother and his home so suddenly, he also found himself living among strangers and having lost his day centre friends, neighbourhood friends, local shops, the garden and his feelings of being wanted, useful and responsible. His first placement was only an emergency temporary one, so this meant another move six weeks later. In his second placement, a health authority centre, he was assessed and came out remarkably low on a test of abilities such as using the telephone, making tea, going shopping and using public transport, although he had been very competent at these skills when he had lived at home. After his assessment he was moved to a local authority social services hostel. This placement was meant to be permanent, but he became very difficult – walking out without permission, shouting at staff and other residents and finally breaking a number of windows; so a case conference was called and resulted in Joe having a fourth move ("because he had failed to settle"). He was sent to a long-stay hospital where he had a few weeks in a locked ward for "difficult" men before moving to an open ward.

Conclusions: Joe's problems were caused by the insensitive management of his bereavement and a lack of forward planning. The professionals made several major mistakes: (a) he was never consulted about his placements; (b) he was assessed at a time when he was unhappy and unsettled; (c) his mother's death took away his feelings of being useful and wanted, and the professionals failed to recognise this loss and provide him with any compensating responsibilities; (d) he was moved away from his neighbourhood and centre, and thus suffered a multitude of other losses; and (e) his multiple moves increased his feelings of insecurity and loss.

The stories of Eva and Joe show how the services provided for bereaved mentally handicapped people can create more problems for them. Such problems occur because many professionals lack information about bereavement and fail to recognise that mentally handicapped people have normal emotional feelings and will suffer normal bereavement reactions.

One of the main aims for any social worker in contact with bereaved mentally handicapped people should be to avoid causing them additional problems on top of their primary grief. To achieve this aim the social worker will need to:

☐ recognise and respect the mentally handicapped person's need to mourn and the normality of their grief;

☐ support them in the changes of life-style caused by a major bereavement, giving special attention to their need for consideration in residential placement;

☐ support widowed parents left caring single-handed for a mentally handicapped person;

☐ try to prepare the family and the mentally handicapped person for changes before a bereavement occurs;

☐ work with other people in contact with bereaved mentally handicapped people.

Following is a discussion of these five tasks.

Recognising and respecting the mentally handicapped person's need to mourn and the normality of their grief. Some social workers may not recognise nor respect mentally handicapped people's right to mourn because they either lack information about normal grief and/or assume that handicapped people do not have the same feelings as more able people.

For example, a social worker who was organising a residential placement for a 25-year-old newly bereaved mentally handicapped man advised the residential care staff that he was "not unduly upset by his father's death because mentally handicapped people do not feel things so deeply as normal people". He was showing normal grief reactions – quietness, disbelief at what had happened, occasional anger, tears, loss of abilities – but, instead of being recognised as grief, his behaviour was thought to be connected with his mental handicap.

A middle-aged woman was admitted to a mental handicap hospital after the death of her sister with whom she had always lived. She showed great distress and the nurses and the social worker recognised her grief. However, they decided to encourage her to join in the hospital's social activities as they believed this would be the best way to help her "get over it". So, a few days after her bereavement, she was told to go to a dance in the hospital recreation hall and to a party and sing-song with a volunteer group.

Although the nurses and the social worker had recognised the woman's grief they made the mistake of not respecting her right to grieve, to be quiet, to cry and to display her sadness by withdrawing from social activities. Bereaved people of normal intelligence would never be expected to immediately enjoy social activities, their right to mourn and be apart from others would be understood and respected; but because this woman had a mental handicap she was "jollied along" in a most insensitive manner.

The above situations might not have occurred if the professionals involved had attended in-service training courses on the recognition of normal grief, and the need to respect the normal feelings of bereaved mentally handicapped people.

Supporting the bereaved mentally handicapped person in the changes of life-style caused by a bereavement, giving special attention to consideration in residential placement. Mentally handicapped people who live at home with widowed parents will probably lose their homes when those widows die. They may be admitted to residential care a few hours after the death. Ideally, their admission should be organised by a social worker they know; and they should go to a residential facility which is familiar to them because they have either stayed there for short-term care or have visited it and met the staff in preparation for one day having to leave home. However, it is quite likely that the social worker who organises the residential care will not know the bereaved mentally handicapped person, and there will be an emergency admission to an unfamiliar hostel or hospital. Sometimes this emergency admission is temporary because it is into a short-term care facility and the bed has been booked for somebody else to have in a few days time. So the grieving person will get moved to another residential facility a few days later, where there will be more new people to meet and another unfamiliar environment.

The research findings suggest that during the first year of a major bereavement a mentally handicapped person is at risk by three moves: the emergency admission; a few days later there is a second move to a temporary placement for an assessment of abilities; and a few months after that there is a third move to a permanent placement.

These moves may be defended by the professionals responsible for them, on the grounds that mentally handicapped people have to be "assessed" so that a decision can be made about their final placement. However, apart from multiple moves being upsetting, it is unwise to assess anyone in the months following a bereavement because people tend to function less efficiently when they are grieving (regardless of whether they are handicapped or very able) so an assessment done during a period of mourning is likely to give a poor impression of anybody's abilities.

Bereaved mentally handicapped people going into residential care will face many strains. If it is their first experience of residential care they will not understand the rules and organisation of the facility, and the difficulties of living in a large group instead of at home with a family. One of their biggest problems will be having to make relationships with staff and residents, at a time when they are sad and not functioning very well and therefore likely to give a poor impression of themselves. And in addition to the main bereavement there will probably be a multiplicity of other losses for the person to contend with. For example, if the residential placement is in a hostel or hospital a long way from the family home, the bereaved person will lose their neighbourhood contacts, local friends, neighbours and familiar shops, and their day centres and the friends they had there amongst the staff and students.

The task for the social worker placing a bereaved mentally handicapped person in residential care does not finish with the placement itself, but should continue with giving him support in adapting himself to his new home; this covers making introductions, helping him to build new relationships, and acting as a friend and advocate. The social worker may have to begin this task by telling the mentally handicapped person the truth about what has happened, explaining his loss, trying to comfort and reassure him that although nobody can replace the dead person, there are other people who will care about him and be his friends. The tragedy is that some mentally handicapped people are not told the truth about what has happened and they continue to believe that their residential placement is temporary and that they will one day return home to their parents.

The social worker may need to point out to the care staff that the bereaved person will need time to mourn and help in realising the loss and the changes in life caused by the death, and then need help in the stages of building up secure memories of the dead person and making new living friendships.

It is important that the loss is faced and the dead person is mourned and then affectionately remembered. The loss and grief should not be avoided in conversation. The dead person and the old home and family life-style were a vital part of the mentally handicapped person's identity so should never just disappear and never be referred to again. The social worker and residential care staff should provide the mentally handicapped person with opportunities to talk about the dead relative. If the person has a speech disability it will be helpful if the social worker and care staff themselves speak of the loss.

Mementos and personal possessions and photographs of family life should always be allowed in residential care. A bereaved middle-aged man in one hostel had his father's old armchair and a large clock in his room; and a young woman in another hostel had pieces of china and pottery and several pictures from home. Sadly, some bereaved mentally handicapped people do not have any mementos of home, nor do they know what has happened to them. It is very important that the social worker, or another familiar professional, should tell the bereaved person what has happened to the family home and their dead parents' belongings. But this does not always happen, the home may be sold up and the mentally handicapped person never know what happened to everything; and even his own personal belongings may be disposed of without consulting him.

The social worker should regularly visit the bereaved mentally handicapped person in the early weeks of the residential care placement. If the care staff never knew the family, the social worker may be able to help by describing the life they led at home. For example, a bereaved mentally handicapped person who was admitted to a hostel after his mother died had a severe speech disability and great difficulty in communicating. Fortunately, the social worker had known him and his mother for several years and after his admission to the hostel she gave him very positive and regular support, acting as his "interpreter" and telling the residential care staff about his life at home so that they could understand his personality and respect his interests. One of his hobbies at home had been collecting all the payout chits that his mother received from the local supermarket and keeping them in envelopes as a form of housekeeping. After the social worker had explained about this, the care staff gave him their chits, and he was able to continue his collecting. If the social worker had not been involved the young man might have become very distressed at not being able to communicate what he wanted and his innocent attempts to explain himself and get some chits (for example, poking at staff purses and getting angry and anxious) may have been interpreted as difficult behaviour.

The social worker may also need to support care staff who become deeply involved in comforting the bereaved person. For example, a young nurse in a mental handicap hospital recognised the need to help a newly admitted bereaved person, and she spent many hours talking with him about his loss, and when she was off duty she arranged to take him to the garden of remembrance. A senior nurse then suggested that she was "getting too emotionally involved" and was impeding his recovery from the loss because she kept talking to him about it and "would not let him forget it". This criticism made her lose confidence in her ability to help people. In such a situation it would be helpful for the social worker to point out to staff at all levels (whether they are nurses or social services care staff), that bereaved people do need individual personal support and staff should help each other in this sensitive task and not be critical about "emotional involvement".

Local authority hostels are often reluctant to accept very severely multiply handicapped people, on the grounds that they have not got the facilities to cope with them. So they are likely to get admitted to long-stay hospital wards when their widowed parents die. Although the nurses may have tried to make the wards homely, they will still seem very strange to somebody admitted from home; the noises, smells, fabrics and lighting will be unfamiliar, and the changes of staff will make it difficult to build up secure relationships. Blind, deaf, multiply handicapped people may be so shocked and bereft at their sudden move from home that they may be prone to illnesses brought on by pining for their caring parent and familiar home environment.

Immediate admission to long-stay hospitals should always be avoided. Social workers may find it necessary to insist that a local authority hostel accepts a multiply handicapped person, or that alternative arrangements are made, such as the person staying for a few weeks in their own home with a care person with them. If there is a desperate shortage of community places and no plans to improve the situation, the social workers may even find it necessary to campaign for better services. "Campaigning" can take many forms – writing a strongly worded report about inappropriate services, bringing up the subject at professional meetings, seeking an interview with the director of social services, helping parents to organise a public meeting about the need for better local services.

Supporting widows who are caring for a mentally handicapped son or daughter. New widows may find it so painful to break the news of a death to their handicapped son or daughter that they resort to stories such as "Dad's still in hospital", or "He's gone to another hospital", or "He's gone on a journey". And some professionals (GPs, teachers, social workers and care staff), actually recommend that the person should not be told the truth because they "will not understand" or "will make a fuss". However, the mentally handicapped person should be told the truth not only because he or she has a right to know the truth and to grieve about it, but also because if elaborate stories are made up about the dead person being "on a journey" or "on holiday", the widows themselves may begin to fantasise that the person has not really died, and their own realisation of the loss may be impeded and this may affect their recovery from the bereavement.

The social worker may need to help the widow break the news of the death to the mentally handicapped person and can continue this help by visiting consistently in the following weeks and encouraging them both to talk about what has happened. It should never be assumed that a person with a severe intellectual handicap and additional language difficulties is incapable of realising what has happened. If the mentally handicapped person cannot speak, he or she will be able to listen to the conversation and share in the widowed parent's grief. It is better to mourn the truth of a death than be made insecure and unhappy because of an unexplained disappearance of a loved member of the family.

Widows often feel that they have been "let down" by social workers. One of their main criticisms is that social workers do not know anything about mentally handicapped people and fail to understand the love that widows feel for their handicapped children.

"*If* they come they obviously don't know anything about handicapped people."

"She just took one look and said I should put him in a hospital and get out more myself."

"This social worker turned up and he didn't seem to understand that I love my child although she's got a dreadful handicap."

The daily tasks of washing, dressing, feeding, carrying, and bathing a profoundly handicapped adult son or daughter are a constant sad reminder of the loss of a married partner. "We did everything together", said one widow, referring to the routines that she and her husband had shared in the many years of caring for their very helpless daughter. Her life-style was completely dislocated by her husband's death. But, in spite of their loneliness and tiredness, the love of widows for their handicapped sons and daughters remains strong and they do not want to be told by social workers that the only answer to their problems is to put that son or daughter away into an institution for long-term care.

The loss of a husband can also mean the loss of the family car and this will increase the widow's isolation, so an important practical way to help widows may be to organise some regular transport for them; for example, a volunteer driver to take the widow and her handicapped son or daughter for pleasant drives and shopping. The mobility allowance may, of course, be used to pay taxi hire but a regular driver has the advantage of offering friendship as well.

The social life of some widows revolves around the activities connected with local groups of parents of handicapped children (MENCAP) where they are sure of a welcome for their son or daughter. Some widows say that they would never have coped without the support of their MENCAP friends. If widowed parents do not belong to a MENCAP group but could be helped by such support and friendship, social workers should put the widow in touch with the local group and help with initial introductions.

Some very lonely widows may rely too much on their mentally handicapped sons and daughters for company, and unintentionally stop them developing adult independence. For instance, the mother of a very competent young man with Down's syndrome resisted the idea of him moving into a council house with a group of three friends because he was her only source of companionship. Social workers must be sensitive to this situation and gently point out to widows that handicapped people have a right to lead independent lives. By leaving the parental home and developing an adult life and a home of their own the handicapped person will be better prepared to cope in the future when both parents have died.

Preparation for loss. Preparation for loss should not be left until the time of a relative becoming terminally ill. It can start early when the family circle is healthy and happy with no impending threat of loss.

If social workers are planning to do any preparatory work on bereavement it is essential that they contact the staff of day centres and special schools who will know about the mentally handicapped person's abilities, their perception of loss and how they have coped with any previous losses. The staff of centres and schools have appropriate opportunities for teaching their mentally handicapped students and pupils about loss, by using stories, films, drama, mime, the death of pets and the death of public figures to illustrate the normality and inevitability of loss and the formal ceremonies that humankind uses to recognise death. Some professionals manage to use their personal experiences to explain loss to their students, unexpectedly finding that their own need for help during a bereavement illustrates how to receive and give sympathy and build up understanding through sharing.

Preparation for loss inevitably raises the question of how much a mentally handicapped person understands about death. It may be said that their understanding is child-like or that they have no understanding at all, but these are unjust generalisations. If they are confused about death it is often because other people give them frightening or incredible information about what has happened; for example they may be told that the dead person has "gone to sleep for ever" or "floated up to the sky". They should always be given the correct words in discussions about death, or when the news of a death is broken to them; for the words "dead", "death", "died" can have only one meaning. Even when a parent or a professional worker suspects that the mentally handicapped person will not fully comprehend these words, they should nonetheless be paid the respect of receiving the truth, and any subsequent support should be built from that starting point.

There are two ways in which social workers can help to prepare mentally handicapped people and their families for loss. First by organising discussions for small groups of parents who are caring for their mentally handicapped children at home; some parents are terrified about their own deaths because they are worried about what will then happen to their handicapped offspring. Discussion groups may help them to bring their fears into the open and start planning for the future; and this may lead on to taking them and their handicapped children to see a residential facility and helping the young people to settle into a new home whilst the parents are still alive. The second way is by talking with mentally handicapped people individually or in a small group about the future, helping them to think about the sort of life they may lead when their parents are no longer there to look after them. Professionals can learn a great deal from listening to the views of mentally handicapped people, at day centres or clubs, and hearing about how they coped with any previous experience of loss and how they have helped each other.

In some instances a social worker may need to take a mentally handicapped person to visit a dying relative in hospital, and it is important that other professionals should not deter them. For example, the sister in charge of a general hospital ward tried to discourage a mentally handicapped man from visiting his dying mother because she thought his presence would upset the mother and other sick patients. Fortunately the social worker insisted on his visiting and she went with him. A year after his mother's death that bereaved man said how much he had appreciated the social worker taking him to the hospital. "She helped me to say goodbye to Mum and I was ready for it when she died," he said.

Perhaps the aim of any preparatory work on loss is to give confidence, the confidence of knowing that although nobody can avoid loss through death, in the pain of the experience there will also be an expectation of support from other people – friends, family and professionals.

Working with other people in contact with bereaved mentally handicapped people. It is important that social workers recognise when the particular skills of other professionals are going to be more appropriate than social work skills. In districts which have well co-ordinated community mental handicap teams the social worker will probably work closely with other professionals

106

who are helping families. The community mental handicap nurses connected with the team may know the family better than the social worker does and be able to give capable support on a long-term basis, including the mentally handicapped person's move into residential care. Most community mental handicap teams have as a member a psychiatrist specialising in the support of mentally handicapped people, and they will be able to advise on any problems related to prolonged grieving.

Many of the problems facing bereaved mentally handicapped people are caused by people treating them in a manner which creates more unhappiness for them. For example, a general practitioner or a district nurse may ask the social worker to arrange short-term care while a parent is dying at home, so the person gets sent away at a time when the family should have remained together. Or an undertaker or clergyman may advise that the handicapped person does not attend the funeral, so the funeral is kept a secret from him but he picks up hints that something is going on that he is not supposed to know about and he becomes deeply upset about it. Of course, some mentally handicapped people would not want to attend a funeral, in the same way as some people who are not handicapped decide that they do not want to. But they should always be given the choice, and other people should not decide on their exclusion without first asking them.

The social worker may have to act as a spokesman for the mentally handicapped person and make sure that people on the periphery (undertakers, vicars, district nurses, GPs and, in the case of sudden death, the police) are sensitive to the person's right to grieve and be included in the sad, absorbing, distressing, but normal formalities of death. It may be necessary to point out that the mentally handicapped person should be given respect, correct information, choice, and support on grief, in the same way as more able people expect such help.

Through contacting local branches of MENCAP and CRUSE, the national organisation for helping widows and their children, social workers may be able to arrange help for widowed parents and also befriending help for bereaved mentally handicapped people who have been admitted to residential care. This will be especially important if the residential facility is a long way from the person's original home and he or she is losing contact with friends from that area. Befriending a bereaved person newly admitted to residential care may include specific tasks connected with the recent bereavement, such as taking them to visit the parents' grave or the garden of remembrance; or may concentrate on helping them adapt to their changed life and make new friends.

Whilst social workers should acquaint themselves with the appropriate local voluntary organisations that might be able to help, care must always be taken to ensure that that voluntary help is consistent. It would be most unfortunate if a bereaved mentally handicapped person was linked to volunteers who soon lost interest and stopped visiting. This would just add a further experience of loss, and cause additional unhappiness.

Lewis, C S *A Grief Observed*. Faber and Faber. 1961.
Parkes, C M *Bereavement*. Tavistock. 1972.
Oswin, M *Holes in the Welfare Net*. Bedford Square Press. 1978.
Pincus, L *Death in the Family*. Faber and Faber. 1976.
Cook, D *Walter*. Penguin. 1980.
Marris, P *Loss and Change*. Routledge and Kegan Paul. 1974.
Wertheimer, A *Living for the Present* CMH Paper No. 9. Campaign for Mentally Handicapped People. 1982.
MENCAP *Bereavement: The formation of a support group in Harrow Weald*. Available from MENCAP, Golden Lane, London EC1.

This chapter is based on the preliminary findings of a research project, financed by the Joseph Rowntree Memorial Fund, into the problems facing mentally handicapped people after a major bereavement.

11

Things of the spirit

Michael Hollings

Some years ago, in the parish where I was living and working, there were several homes for elderly people. One which I frequently visited had a male assistant matron who over the months since his arrival had either glared at me or studiously avoided me. I was truly surprised one day when the 'phone rang and the voice on the other end announced that the assistant matron was speaking and would I come round for a talk! On my arrival, he said he wanted me to be clear about two things. First, he was an atheist. Second, he intensely disliked Roman Catholics. As I was and am a Roman Catholic and I believe in God, this was a good opening! However, he went on to say that with every old person there came a time when medical treatment could do no more and when nursing could not save them from death. Would I, he asked, take over from there onwards as I had something to give that they had not?

In fact, a useful, happy and fruitful friendship grew from there, so that gradually he came to see that I could be more effective in the long term if I was about earlier, getting to know the men and women, breaking down barriers of tension and so on.

I give this incident, because the question of religion in sickness, terminal illness, death and bereavement is an awkward one for some people. Probably, it is true to say that there has been a considerable shift in position in the past 20 to 30 years. By that I mean in hospitals and among social workers in the early part of my priestly life in the 1950s I often found my presence was considered unnecessary and even intrusive. I was seldom approached by a social worker on any point or with any request for help. Perhaps they saw no point in my involvement.

More recently, there has been considerable change. This may partly be my age, but I think the climate also has changed. Today, there is much more widespread interest in religion, even when there is, perhaps, less practice. Meditation of one sort or another is quite widespread. Also the rise of "alternative medicine" has suggested that such meditation, relaxation and the like may be more therapeutic than the continued use of many drugs. In addition, too, it has been realized that the psychological effects of the "stiff upper lip", the suppression of grief, can have a very harmful effect.

Looked at in a pragmatic way, it is clear that there has been a huge fall off in church attendance in this century. But despite this, opinion poll after opinion poll over the years comes out with high statistics for those who believe in God in some way, even though doing nothing about it. Interestingly, belief has been augmented considerably by those who have come to the British Isles from overseas. Many of these are Christian, but those who are not include ardent followers of the great world faiths, the Hindu, Muslim, Sikh and Buddhist, to name the outstanding ones.

I strongly suggest that the existence of religious belief in others is an important part of the awareness of a social worker. Whether or not the social worker has religious belief, the client may be very deeply influenced personally, or his family may be. Where there is religious belief, it can be a positive strength in bereavement.

Now, it does not mean that the social worker has to take on this aspect of the client. But it is necessary to acknowledge it and to see what care can be taken of it. This can be done by familiarity with the local church leaders, knowing how and where to contact them and whether there are neighbourhood sisters or church workers available to help. Naturally, what I am writing does not only apply to bereavement, but is a much longer-term suggestion, because there are many other vicissitudes in life when the active assistance of the church and voluntary organisations can be invaluable to a hard-pressed case-loaded social worker. There can be present a network of caring people who visit, give lifts in cars, do odd jobs and in some cases bring holy communion to the housebound or hold little Bible or prayer services in individual rooms, flats or houses.

Attitudes to death and after-life

It is important as an assistance to the social worker and the families concerned, that the varying customs and beliefs of different religious groups are recognised and supported.

Christian views and those of world faiths on death and after-life vary considerably but generally speaking, there is quite clear foundation teaching. The interpretation or degree to which that teaching is held or comprehended differs.

I have to generalise but by and large, all Christian teaching firmly adheres to the doctrine of life after death. There is only one death – there is no coming back, no reincarnation, no second chance. The teaching is that this after-life is somehow with God in a place of peace, joy and love, where there will be complete happiness forever – heaven. But some churches more than others, emphasize the possibility of a wicked person failing to "qualify" for this bliss, owing to sin, and that his destiny is hell. Very often the picture painted is one of reward or punishment, depending upon the life of the person here and now, his faith and for some the amount he does for others – his good works. This means that for some whose religion has become a bit guilt-ridden, there can be real fear of the wrath of God beyond the grave, while for others there will be (behind the fear of the process of dying and the loss of contact with family and friends here) a real and deep joy in the hope of meeting the God of love.

Interestingly, until more recent times, there had grown the practice of a conspiracy of silence which did its best to conceal the approach of death from the dying person – and even from relatives. To some extent this was supported (and perhaps still is) by doctors whose profession it is to cure, and whose pride it is not to admit defeat in the face of even terminal illness. Such a policy leads to living a lie towards someone who is dying, with empty remarks about recovery: "You *are* looking better today"! It is also taking a poor view of the character of human nature to think it cannot take knowledge of its impending death without some breakdown or despair.

For Roman Catholics, especially, there is the particular sacrament of anointing of the sick. This can be given to a person in danger of death through illness. Its nature is twofold in the Church's teaching: it is healing from sickness and sin, and it is also preparatory to the last journey of death. In the case of a Roman Catholic, therefore, the introduction of a priest and the giving of the anointing can be spiritually, mentally and psychosomatically very helpful. Other Christian churches are not always so specific about the anointing, though many today have healing services and the laying on of hands.

Jews have always had a strong belief in the after-life, although as with Christianity, this can get eroded by secularism. The teaching of resurrection from the dead has also been normal except among the Sadducees. As a family religion with strong and ancient loyalties, the support of family and the home religious element are important, but involvement is very particularly Jewish. It is not so easy for the gentile to penetrate or to be of much help, perhaps. In a way, I found, the most important aspect is to know Jewish customs and to be available, if necessary, in any way of service.

Muslims are strongly monotheistic and have very specific rules and law laid down in the Qur'am (or Koran). They believe in the uniqueness of death and in the resurrection of the body. Because of this, burial and not cremation is the law, with the top of the grave standing some inches above the level of the earth surrounding it. They sometimes need help with cemetery authorities to ensure this slight elevation.

Hindus believe in the transience of the soul from the body to a new existence in this world. For them, more than for many other religions, there is a certain acceptance of the inevitability of death which leads on, not to resurrection, but to reincarnation.

111

Hindus cremate their dead and where possible like the ashes scattered into a river, as is done *par excellence* in the Ganges. I have found that they appreciate the presence of those other than Hindus at their funeral ceremonies.

Sikhs also normally use cremation, but there is nothing in Guru Monok's writing to lay down specific funeral rites. So, although cremation is normal, the Sikh can vary according to the custom of the country in which he lives.

Before the crematorium ceremony there is usually a service in the home. A dead body is not allowed in the Gurdwara, the Sikh place of worship. At home the coffin is opened, and fruit, flowers and sweetmeats put in. In England cremation is used, and the men of the family will insist upon viewing the coffin in the furnace, after it has been removed from the crematorium chapel.

As a believer, I accept that every man, woman and child is created out of God's love, is individually unique, and has the promise of life after death. But I also believe that they are free. This means that I hold what I hold and that I have the right to express my belief. But I have no right to *impose* my belief. My approach, then, varies from person to person. With some, I know that they are Roman Catholic and I am a priest. But they may or may not *want* any church contact. Some years ago, because I had been in the army, I was asked by a hospital matron to visit an old soldier who had had a trachieotomy. We talked for six months of everything except religion. After that he wrote on his pad one day: "Next time I want to see you as a priest."

Where possible getting to know the family is vital, because to me they often need as much support as the dying person. There is the problem – should he be told? There is the other problem – should relations be told? Again, I cannot over-ride anyone if there is a veto on knowing the truth, but nevertheless my general endeavour is to work towards knowledge. I believe this is more in keeping with human dignity, that there may well be things in a person's life which need to be sorted out, and that often family relationships can grow and deepen in a beautiful way by sharing in the terminal period fully.

Not only that, when death comes, though it is no easier, it is something already foreseen, discussed and partly shared. The last days or weeks, together in knowledge, are a wonderful source for the recollection at the bereavement which can bring tears, healing and even joy.

Therefore I like to begin getting closer as early as possible when someone is dying. Naturally this takes time and patience. It is important, also, if the person is in the ward of a hospital to spread oneself if possible – that is not simply to concentrate on him at the beginning, unless that is wanted.

The advantage or disadvantage a priest or religious sister has is the visibility of what they are which can be accepted or rejected; but is often associated with the ultimates – spirit, sickness, death. The social worker has other more immediate points of contact which can be used. But this *may* keep the relationship to a shallower or more businesslike level.

In my experience, I have been approached by families, hospital staff and social workers when they felt that there is a dimension of care which is not quite in their experience or field of work. Sometimes, too, the sheer time factor is one which makes deep contact difficult. In my own work, apart from terminal care and bereavement, I am constantly referring people and situations to social workers, because they have both the background and backing of the social services, and expertise which I lack. Equally I would like to think that there are areas where social workers could value the involvement of a priest or minister or church worker.

There is one other time factor – the weekend and the holiday periods. Quite rightly, the social worker has a five day week. The resident local clergy may be particularly busy on Saturday and Sunday, but usually they are still in the area. For either the person dying at home or the bereaved, the weekend and especially times like Easter (Thursday, Friday and Monday) and Christmas and New Year (sometimes with the holiday break of about two weeks) can be very lonely and long drawn-out. It is also normally a fact that the clergy do not have "hours", so that weekday evenings can also be times when some support can be given.

It is true, as in other areas, that those likely to suffer most are the more reserved, less open, longer established residents of these islands. Newer arrivals both from West and East and also from Europe are less "private" and far less inhibited about death. Generally speaking they are also more familiar with religious after-life concepts.

Where there is no religious belief and not always much neighbourly or family closeness, it is not easy to penetrate into situations of grief and bereavement, or to bring out new life. Occasionally the street or a local body comes to the rescue, but in my experience a great deal may depend in these cases upon the gentle patience and persuasiveness of the social worker. A believing social worker can pray for the individual and, without proselytising or abusing the working relationship, can give some strength and support through her own personal faith. If there is acquaintance, friendship or even a working relationship with a minister of religion or church worker, whether the social worker believes or not, advice should be freely sought if needed – and I hope freely given. However it is necessary to point out that clergy, religious sisters and lay people can individually or in groups have very different viewpoints – in other words, it is safer to know or know about the "professional" cleric and others, to be able to sum him up, before asking advice or seeking help.

Once death has occurred there are two immediate concerns – the funeral arrangements and the support of the bereaved. The funeral arrangements, unfortunately, are surrounded by red tape in the form of death registration, certificates, undertaker's details, cemetery or cremation availability. Some, especially the elderly people – and especially poor widows – are not only stunned by the death of the one they love, but also completely at sea about what to do. The death and registration is routine for officialdom. It can be a nightmare for the relative: removal of the body if it is at home or the visit to hospital to collect personal belongings and the death certificate; taking the certificate to the registrar – who may possibly be a long way off, and the need to wait in a queue; eventually see the undertaker; considering the costs, burial or cremation, and possibly church arrangements.

I have often found the first genuine way of helping is accompanying the bereaved person on the rounds, advising on funeral arrangements, as well as listening at various long waits to the necessary reminiscences about the beloved. Most people scarcely have time to manage this amount of time. I think the minister of religion often has. Also, most funerals and cremations are still taken by a minister. How much nicer it is when that minister already, before the service, has contact with some of the family. He can pop round to the home, talk to the undertaker, discuss the service.

The bereaved sometimes seeks solitude, but I think more often needs someone about and a listening ear. Platitudes of sorrow are normally useless: encouragements to cheer up are out of place. A presence, a capacity to listen, the freedom to comfort with a hug or to sit close beside with an arm round the shoulders – these little nothings are immensely reassuring. Also, for some, making the funeral arrangements and planning to entertain those mourners are helpful occupations. They give the bereaved a sense of still being able to care about the beloved, making a contact even across the coffin, not finally losing touch yet, not being totally inadequate and useless.

Some ethnic groups have very good support systems. Those from the West Indies, for instance, come together amazingly quickly in the house of the bereaved, often the same evening. From then until the funeral, every evening or night, the house or a single room will be crowded. With or without a minister or priest, there will be praying, hymn singing, conversation and some liquid refreshment. Sometimes the Irish families have the same routine, though less today than in the past. It is, in my experience, the English, not a very religious people, who need more care because they are less backed by traditional family and religious community. Here especially, the social worker may be left to lead or build a support group, because in England it seems to be customary to shun death in the street, leaving the bereaved alone, through respect or shyness, sometimes because of fear of not knowing what to say.

One feeling which hits the bereaved in many cases is guilt. It is natural for us when facing death and bereavement, to go over in our minds our whole relationship with the one we are to lose or have already lost. In a sense, we can never do enough for one we love. That part of us which goes deeper than sexual attraction, friendship, companionability, family relationship and so on, touches us at a point I would call spiritual.

This guilt does not only dig at those who have been truly selfish, neglectful or downright cruel. It can severely attack a most loving parent, a devoted husband or wife, a son or daughter who has in a way sacrificed personal life to remain living and caring for a widowed parent. It is to be hoped that in most cases this guilt will gradually assume a minor position – but at first it can be very destructive, turning a person in on self in condemnation and in bitter regret at lack of love given, taking blame for the illness and death, eaten up with remorse which now cannot be assuaged by any direct restitution. Once again reassurance or an attempt to contradict this guilt-feeling are largely useless. It is best to sit and let it pour out, so that some of the poison evaporates. A believer can still pray for the dying or deceased person. When a family is involved, the continuance and development of the family can be a life-line to help work through the guilt.

Perhaps the main thing from a worker's point of view is to accept the naturalness of this reaction, so as to be able to live with it, accept it, and even take the bitterness out of it through listening and through helping to positive resurrection.

Though there is immediate need after death, there is in many ways greater need in the follow-through after the funeral is over. There is a great finality about the coffin being lowered into the ground or the crematorium doors shutting the coffin from view. Return home – some food perhaps – people gathering – condolences – then night and the morning after and life stretching ahead. For many this is when emptiness and loneliness strike hardest and deepest.

As a Christian, I see the cycle in our life as being one of living, dying and rising again. We each of us live in friendship and love; when that dies, we die to a degree; then we are to rise again to the next part of life, which will be new and different, without the former love. Beautiful as it is in many ways to centre life still on the one who has died, it is no disrespect to the dead for us to go on living, to break new ground, to find fresh joy. Christians and others have in the past emphasized mourning. Today we realise it is much more in keeping with the resurrection to come out of our emotional entombment and live again fully. As the women at Christ's tomb were told: "Why look among the dead for someone who is alive?"

It is necessary for the bereaved person to give vent to grief, but not so good to prolong it and wallow in it. Both spiritually and psychologically a gradual move to a new life is most important. Here the loved one is not discarded, but rather remains a memory and a background against which the new future is painted. I have heard it said often that it may take six months, a year, even 18 months for a particular individual to surface from grief. This process of rising can be helped; it must not be hurried.

I write from where I am personally and try to share some of the thoughts and experiences which I have had over some 37 years of work as a priest, mostly in city surroundings. I can imagine from recollections of my boyhood that the smaller country and village community may be closer and more caring than parts of the inner city or suburbia. But then, just for the reason of the complex and isolating influences of urban living, the number of social workers is probably greater in cities than in the countryside.

Social work is about professional care and concern and work for the *whole* person, man, woman or child. Therefore, while I have been stressing what I was asked to write about – "the spiritual dimension" – I believe that this chapter really merges into any and every other chapter. When we are associating with each other, we can ordinarily have a "business relationship", a "professional", "academic", "psychiatric", or "platonic" relationship. But for the growth and settlement in themselves and in the community, individuals and families need as complete and rounded an assistance and understanding as is possible.

Whatever anyone may believe or profess in reference to God, the after-life and so on, it is clear that the human being is very complex. There is that "life" keeping us in being, which is more than a mere winding up of a clock and its slow running down. This element of the spiritual or the psyche, the person or the intellectual, is a necessary part of the approach to and working with any client or case.

We can each of us approach a task from the same origin, or we can have almost entirely different backgrounds, or we can be anywhere between the two extremes. It is very important and useful for ordinary people who are at risk in one way or another, that there should be as much working together between different agencies as possible, so that we continue to try to build healthy and happy people, who live the full term of their lives; and then come through sickness to a dignified and peaceful death, while their relations and friends share in this last period of relationship in this world, and then build together a new life following the death of the beloved one.

THOSE WHO ARE LEFT

12

The spirit cannot die

Bel Mooney

Speech after long silence, I find myself driven to return to a subject I thought I had left behind. The compulsion has much to do with the time of year: November, with its damp leaves, wind and desolation and the sense of falling forward into darkness. With this comes an unavoidable sense of anniversary. For though I may attempt to deflect, and to keep at bay through frantic activity, it is impossible to avoid remembering something which happened ten years ago this month. Defiantly, I wonder why I should thus apologise for the fact, to myself as well as to you. So – no apologies. It happened. It was a death: a very small death, but a death for all that.

For it was in November 1975, after 15 hours of labour and at full term, that my second son was born dead. Not long afterwards I wrote about the event for *The Guardian*, an article which had an astonishing effect. Letters flooded in from those who had also suffered this strange and (then) unspoken of bereavement, which is birth and death in one. As a direct result of that readers' response an organisation called the Stillbirth Association was formed, which still flourishes; later, the Health Education Council published a booklet; slowly, attitudes began to change and hospital staff showed a much greater understanding . . . But none of that concerns me now. All of it was a long time ago, but there is still something left to set down; that all of us, in our understandable and selfish terror, underestimate the capacity of death to have a profound, positive and lasting effect on life itself.

Let me say hastily that it is not large-scale death of which I speak, not the result of war, famine, catastrophe or outrage, but the simple, ordinary, individual death which each one of us has to confront – sooner or later. Though each death will be different and experienced in raw freshness each time (the death of a child, the death of a friend, the death of a beloved parent), the first response is usually anger – a railing against the heavens for allowing this to happen. It would be astonishing were that not so. When (for example) a distinguished man dies at the "early" age of 48, after courageously fighting a terrible illness for several years – a man at the height of his powers with a great future cut short and a wife and two growing children left bereft, then any of his friends will hear of his death with impotent rage. Why should such a man lie dead when all around the mean, the idle, the corrupt, the inadequate, the ignorant, the brutal, thrive in their health and strength? Each day, somewhere, somebody reiterates Lear's long scream of agony at the unfair absurdity of it: "Why should a horse, a dog, a rat have life, and thou no breath at all?"

Close cousins to such indignant pity for the dead are the understandable self-pitying questions of those left behind: "Why *me*? What have *I* done to deserve this?" There is no answer to either cry. Yet we can stumble towards a "hint half understood" by means of one simple, yet devastating and demanding exercise. Instead of "Why?", turn the question on its head, and ask: "Why not?". That is the essence, the mystery.

For although you may hate the fact of death, you can still, simultaneously, accept that it has to be; it is also possible to take this a step further, going beyond mere passive acceptance, and seeking instead to discover what results from the pain. Fear is the first thing – and it might as well be accorded full import. *Timor mortis conturbat me*, uniting us with those medieval men who were terrified into living virtuously by the vision of the death's head: the prospect of worms eating the body, hellfire devouring the soul. Now – when the first consumes the body and there is only vacancy for the soul – the fear is worse. An article by the novelist A N Wilson (published in the *Spectator*) seemed to me to be evidence of this. In a straight-talking attempt to be strong-minded, to confront the "facts of death", it confused nervous, schoolboyish callowness with honesty – symbolised most jarringly by the repeated use of the word "stiffs", for dead bodies. It was about the pathology of death – only one infinitesimal part of its mystery and truth; and it was suffused with revulsion and horror.

All my life, *until* my child was stillborn, I would have shared that fear, and shouted with rage against the "dying of the light". I would quote, with approval, Simone de Beauvoir's words: "There is no such thing as a natural death: nothing that happens to a man is ever natural since his presence calls the world into question. All men must die; but for every man his death is an accident, and even if he knows it and consents to it, an unjustifiable violation" (1969).

Now . . . I am not so sure about the truth of that stirring arrogance. It may serve to explain the courage of the dying, but is there not a danger that it also explains it away? An even more familiar and over-quoted phrase is also perturbing: "Any man's death diminishes me." Donne's great meditation still reaches out across centuries with its plea for fellowship, for compassion. Yet it, too, may be questioned. Why should any man's death necessarily diminish? To witness a death borne courageously, to read of heroism and death in the face of persecution . . . does that not *enhance*? There is a serious case for saying that *every* man's death adds to me, if I allow it; and far from being a violation, death may be a consummation – although not devoutly wished. To put it another way: it is life that we diminish by turning away in such horror from its ending, for (in Jung's phrase) waxing and waning are part of the same curve.

I know no greater expression of this idea than Schubert's String Quartet in D minor, known as "Death and the Maiden". Schubert, fated to live the pitifully small span of 31 years, leaving works of beauty and majesty unfinished, not even having had the chance to hear most of his chamber music performed – Schubert understood death even before it came. In the song "Der Tod und Madchen" the young girl is appalled to find death near, saying she is not ready for him. The reply of the reaper is tender: "Be of good courage, I am not wild, you will slumber gently in my arms."

In the variations on these bars in the quartet, we can hear the eternal dialogue plainly. It is like someone walking out into the deep, feeling the undertow pull, the swell of death start to lift and carry away, only to turn for a moment and scrabble wildly in the direction of the departing shores of life . . . before turning back and accepting the end. The final mood is not tragic, but relentlessly exciting – as though by turning to face the spectre face to face we see, for the first time in that dreaded visage, a strength and a sweetness which we recognise proudly as our own. What we were born to.

Coming to terms with the idea of one's own death is hard but essential; only then is it possible to contemplate with any equanimity the death of those one loves. And I would interrupt all the wise phrases of bereavement counselling, all the talk of "loss", with this blunt truth: that when someone you love dies you might as well accept the fact that you will be haunted by that person for the rest of your life. A proper *haunting* – that is what I have known for ten years, but have only just realised. Each year, at this time, I have imagined my baby growing, changing, experiencing the stages of school, friendship, fun – a vision that is in stark contrast to the reality: the cremation I did not attend, and the ashes I never saw scattered on rosebushes. That is not morbid; it simply invested what happened with permanent dignity. And nor do I mind it any more – "the third who walks always beside" . . . because without the sum total of ten years' imagining I would certainly be the lesser person.

It is a blithe spirit indeed, and I do not want it exorcised. From corpses and "stiffs", through spooks and ghosts, we arrive in the land of spirits, and that linguistic journey is a lesson in reverence and lack of fear. It involves a willingness to love the dead for what they are – the *Manes*, the souls of the departed, for whom we go on living, doing all the things they could not do, and allowing them to add to the whole of what *we* are.

In the multiplicity of grief I do not compare mine with that of parents I have met at Great Ormond Street Hospital, or the widow of the man cut down in his prime. Yet all of us – angry, demented, guilty, bitter, released, disappointed or however we may respond – have this in common: we are placed permanently on the interface between suffering and acceptance, and weighed with the knowledge that death is simultaneously an individual agony and the most unarguable testimony to ordinary, sublime humanity. The grief goes on – and there is a very good reason for this permanence. In the words of Franz Marc: "The spirit cannot die – in no circumstances, under no torment, despite whatever calumnies, in no bleak place."

And nor can it ever be forgotten amid the mundanity of everyday life, and of ambition, achievement and age. It is that – not a source of pain but of wonder – which I have been taught by my little ghost of ten winters.

de Beauvoir, S *A Very Easy Death*. Penguin. 1969.

13

Learning from the dying person and relatives

Alison Wertheimer

In the autumn of 1984, my mother was dying of cancer in a large London teaching hospital. She had been admitted to that hospital while we waited for a bed to become vacant at the nearest hospice. When a place did become available there, she was moved, and died within 24 hours of her arrival. I still breathe a sigh of relief that she didn't die in that large teaching hospital. Perhaps we were just unlucky with that particular hospital (although it was ironic that my mother had chosen to work there as a nurse for five years until she retired). But I am still left wondering how they managed to get so much so wrong, when the hospice, even in the short time we were there, managed to get so much right. And I'm still wondering whether it's really only hospices that can provide good terminal care.

When you're going somewhere probably to die, how you are treated when you arrive at that place, seems incredibly important. Leaving her home for the last time wasn't easy for my mother, in spite of the gentle kindness of the ambulance crew, but our arrival at the hospital did nothing to lessen our collective depression. Despite the fact that the admission had been arranged earlier that day, the bed wasn't ready and we were told we'd have to wait before being allowed up to the ward. So we spent a miserable half-hour, stuck in a corner of the very busy casualty department. Doctors and nurses rushed around, but no one took any notice of us – until I insisted that we should be taken up to the ward.

When we finally arrived, we were taken into a gloomy single room. It wasn't very clean, but worse still, the bedside call bell wasn't working. As my mother's illness meant she could by then only whisper, she would have been helpless if left alone.

For the next few hours, nurses dashed briefly in and out, never stopping to talk for long, but throwing out cheery remarks like: "Oh good, now you're back we can feed you up a bit." Maybe they hadn't read her notes, and maybe they didn't notice she was dying, but the feeble jokes and lack of awareness of her situation made her, and me, very angry. It took five hours for a doctor to come and see her, so during that time she was not allowed any medication. The doctor was young and rather nervous. He didn't want to prescribe anything much, he told her, "in case you get used to it". (I suppose they could have written "drug addiction" on the death certificate instead of "cancer". Would it have mattered?) When my father and brother arrived that evening, I thankfully escaped.

Over the next two days, my mother, who had been calm and peaceful before we arrived at the hospital, became increasingly angry and depressed. Misery was compounded by a sense of isolation; it seemed as though the staff were unable or unwilling to share in what we were going through. On a busy hospital ward, maybe the staff don't have too much time to talk, but it was hard not to feel that we were receiving little attention because there wasn't much they felt they could offer a dying patient. At one point I did suggest to one of the doctors that it would be better for everyone when we could move my mother to the hospice. Her response that "we do deal with it here, you know" didn't leave me feeling any more optimistic about their ability to do more than "deal" with death and I felt distinctly uneasy about how they would cope with us as bereaved relatives.

Perhaps it's hard for hospitals when they can't actively "treat" people any more; but there were so many small things they could have done which would have made a world of difference. The offering of food, for example, has always been one of the ways we can show care for another person. My mother didn't want or need very much to eat by then, but when a full portion of not very attractively served food was just slapped down on a table – often out of her reach – she usually ended up not touching most of the meal. Not that anyone seemed to mind, despite all the talk about "feeding her up".

Being a visitor in hospital is, at the best of times, a strange experience, but sitting by my mother's bed, I began to wonder if I was invisible. I used to arrive at about breakfast-time on the ward. Sometimes a nurse would say "hello", but otherwise nobody really seemed to acknowledge my presence. I wasn't even sure I was supposed to be there outside the official visiting hours. No one questioned me, so I stayed, but a positive welcome would have been nice. Although I was sometimes there for seven or eight hours, no one suggested I might like to use the hospital dining facilities which must have existed. I suppose I could have eaten my mother's untouched meals though I'm sure that would have been against the rules; it felt demeaning enough having to beg the occasional cup of tea or coffee from the trolley lady.

Two days before my mother died I came on to the ward to find her utterly defeated. Convinced that she wouldn't make it to the hospice where a bed was available the next day, and barely able to hold a pen, she wrote a note, insisting that I give it to one of the nurses. She begged them to "let her go", saying: "I can't stand it any longer". I'm pretty sure that it wasn't physical pain that was troubling her but I couldn't explain to the staff that it was the emotional pain of the last few days that had brought her to write that note.

It was a young student nurse who dealt with my tears, calmed my mother down, and told me that she'd give up nursing the day she stopped caring about her patients. It was the first time I felt anyone in that huge institution really cared about what we were going through – and then only when it had reached a crisis point.

Our arrival at the hospice the next day was in marked contrast to our hospital admission earlier that week. Matron came into the ambulance itself, and taking my mother's hand said: "We are so glad you have chosen to come and be with us." And after that there was no waiting around; my mother's bed was waiting for her just inside the door, warmed with a hot-water bottle.

We were taken straight up to the ward, which turned out to be a series of pleasant single rooms, where we were both immediately offered coffee and biscuits. At the same time, staff came in and introduced themselves to us and helped us to settle in. I say "us" because that was how it felt at the hospice. There wasn't just a "patient", but a dying person and her family who were all involved in what was happening.

A doctor arrived within half an hour for what was as much a chat as a consultation. It was so unlike one brief visit we'd had in hospital where a consultant she didn't know (her own consultant was away that week) had come in and, without introducing herself, had rather roughly examined my mother and disappeared again. This doctor was completely different. He said straightaway to my mother: "I can see you're very tired and breathless", so he examined her only briefly and very gently. But even more importantly, in that first conversation we were able to share with him and the nursing staff the fact that my mother almost certainly had very little time to live. And as the doctor said, "I promise you, you will not die in pain here, and you will not die alone", it was wonderful to see the earlier calmness returning to her face. Feeling so supported by the hospice staff, it was possible to be open to the fact of her impending death.

As soon as she had seen the doctor, morphine and anti-emetic drugs were given without having to wait, and after another visit, this time from the chaplain (my mother was a practising Anglican), she was served with lunch. The meal was small and dainty and served so nicely she was able, for the first time in days, to almost finish the meal.

There was no question of my sitting hungry by the bedside. I was invited to go down to the dining-room with the nurses and my offer of payment for the excellent meal was gently but firmly refused. Hospice hospitality is an important part of their philosophy, and it is a hospitality which extends to families as well as patients.

I left my mother later that afternoon. I felt exhausted but

perfectly confident that she was somewhere at last where she felt comfortable and secure. After spending an evening with an old friend, I came home and fell into bed and had the best sleep for days. But I was woken by the phone ringing at about 4 a.m. It was the hospice saying that my mother's breathing had changed and they thought my father and I should come over straight-away. But they couldn't contact my father. That was their only mistake: they had written my father's phone number down wrongly. So we both arrived there minutes after she had died. But at least, as they had promised, she had died with someone with her until the very end.

I went back to the hospice later that day to face what I had dreaded most, which was seeing a dead person for the first time in my life. But again the hospice staff were extremely supportive. A nurse from my mother's ward came down and offered to come into the chapel with me. We sat outside and talked and then went in together to see my mother. I don't think I could have done it on my own (and I wondered later whether the hospital would have been able to spare a nurse to come with me). In fact it was all easier than I had anticipated. The body seemed like an empty shell. The nurse reminded me that if I wanted to touch her she would feel cold – but I decided not to, preferring to remember the warm hand I'd held the day before.

My father, brother and I were all offered unlimited time and support from the hospice staff that day – and afterwards. There was no sense of being "cut off" just because my mother was no longer alive. So my brother was able to take our 99-year-old grandmother to see the place where her daughter had died. My father returned on one or two occasions, including a special service for people from my mother's ward and a tea with the staff afterwards. I have myself been back on several occasions, usually to talk to my mother's doctor who is an infinitely wise and caring person.

But the sad fact remains that only a small fraction of the population does die in a hospice setting – about five per cent, I believe. Many more people will die in hospital. But I'm sure that some of what we experienced in the hospice could have been replicated in hospital. Hospices have been able to teach the hospitals a great deal about matters like pain control. But a different sort of learning is needed too – about how it feels to be a dying patient and about how it feels to be a relative facing imminent loss and bereavement. In my mother's case we were lucky – but only just. Others may not be so lucky.

14

A past and future, too

Diana Davenport

I make a subjective scrutiny of grief and loss – and find a bed of mingled sensations: emotions as far removed, one from the other, as the sharpest anguish and a still white calm. Twelve months, a whole year since my son Sebastian died. Killed himself. Killed himself without fuss: without any weakness or "crying for help", and with the single-minded certainty that he was joining his beloved girl – herself killed while cycling to work four months previously. Already its been too long a time for even the closest of friends to treat one still with everyday tenderness; too short a time to get through so much as a single waking hour without meeting up with his dear ghost around some mental corner.

Mourning him (mourning them both) has wrought change in me, turned me inwards a good deal, abstracted the mind. I see those early weeks after his death – back further even to the earliest days – and am angry and disappointed with myself for the dumb inertia. I sense an eye half-shielded from reality and a body half-anaesthetised against pain: hence the great and overwhelming lassitude which, while keeping the outward and visible within conventional bounds, also blunted shamefully the edges of my courage, which I needed in order to do the things I wanted to do before those chances vanished for ever.

Lowered almost to the subserviency of childhood, I waited within my amorphous limbo for both friend and stranger to read my mind. To suggest – to ask – would I (for instance) like to cut a curl of his dark hair to keep? Yes . . . yes . . . how I long for it *now*, when it's been burned away all this time: the filaments of his being – burned. How, too, I remember longing to step forward in that crematorium's chapel, just to put a hand on his coffin before the final going away: a soft and comforting Godspeed. Yet, rigid with conformity and Valium, I stood with the rest, with only my mind stretching out.

One of my dearest friends, whose son died at the same time, though a year before Baz, reiterates this regret for not salvaging a lock of hair. So listen, all understanding friends and professionals, and heed for future reference. Take scissors to your quiet chapel: remember that people full of sorrow are often dumbstruck. *Ask* her if she'd like a snip of hair. Give her a chance. Give *him* a chance, too, because men, especially in this our Rambo society, are not as free to show anguish as are we women.

Then afterwards, of course, there are the ashes. The ashes in their incongruous plastic container (rather like a cider jar) and their sober cardboard box. Signed for, handed over, they are ours. Do we have another little service and put them in a scaled-down grave? Do we scatter them among the flowers and shrubs in the garden? Do we toss them into wind and weather from a favourite Suffolk cliff-top or from the midst of a loved stone circle?

Society, on the whole, suggests that we get rid of these precious ashes in order, almost, that we might seal the death; be done with the practical matters. And, of course, whether I speak for the great majority of grieving people, or whether I speak only on account of my own hugely possessive mother-love, I cannot know, but, for me, the idea of letting go, of consigning Baz's grey powder to earth or air, was a step almost impossible to contemplate. I really do believe that, had anyone suggested I make a sort of heavenly porridge of those ashes, I would have done so – and with all the urgency of a she-wolf intent upon devouring her young to "keep them safe". Such was the massive drive to hang on to all that remained, the phrenetic fight even as I sieved through the coarse grains for any recognisable scrap, however minuscule, which might have escaped the crusher; *any* diminutive fragment would do. Yet, from the other side of this nightmare, nagged the little granule of objective sanity left to me: Baz must be *seen* to make his final earthly move to Suze. Their ashes must mingle as one.

The mind goes back to another old friend of mine who, widowed at sixtyish, took her late husband's underclothes to bed with her for the remainder of her days, an eccentricity I used to treat with private amusement but which now, caught myself in the squirrel-wheel of grief, I can perfectly understand. I who, on the night before Baz's crumbs were left with his beloved Suze's (under a beech tree in her mother's garden), slept with that brown jar of ashes clasped to my bosom, possessed of a wild and irrational desire to warm them up. I who, unable even at the eleventh hour to let go completely, quietly removed a handful of all that remained to keep for myself.

Yet time passes. A sense of perspective begins to layer itself over my private search for scraps of material reassurance. The cinema screen of his life plays echoes in my head – a repeated game of "Do-you-recall?". His young friends have, in many instances, become my friends and I know that some of them, at least, understand how important they have become to me as (in a way) the tail of Baz's bright comet. With them I am able to talk about this lost boy – they who were so close to him. Talk to them in a way which is not possible, say, with older friends – who often cannot separate Baz's boistrous past from the solemnity and pity of his death. And sometimes it is necessary to laugh.

Many, still, are the stalwarts to whom death is a conversational avenue not to be trodden. Talk about anything to poor old Diana, but don't mention her son: steer her mind on towards politics or the Women's Institute or the state of the drains – but steer clear of the hereafter. Oh, can't they realise that I *want* to speak of him, want their soft and stumbling words, that there is no embarrassment?

Events cannot be reversed. Death cannot be undone. The reality of existing within a truncated family has to be faced and dealt with. Externally I am not all that different. Perhaps a little dowdier, quieter, less of a goer-out. Inwardly I am tired almost to the point of falling asleep at 9.30 in the morning, haunted by the tragedy of Baz and Suze, hungry for dreams.

I am learning that the experience of grief is long and slow. It pushes one back so that a mist rises between thought and action. Life separates onto two concurrent planes – the spiritual hunt for proof that all is well, and the daily business of "carrying on". Carrying on, yes, even when I come across this comb of his – as I did just now – and scrupulously go over it for the gift of just one dark hair. But find none.

I write again to clarify my path of grief. The second year is almost gone. I cry less, can trust myself to go out, can laugh and temporarily lose myself in a Baz-less world. His poems I cannot yet read without tears; cannot ride my bicycle without giving him a weather report or telling him to look at the sun on the hills or the evening clouds stringing themselves with red; cannot get rid of the irrational urge to ring him up. There are things, events, of which I can write now but could not last year: the dream in particular. Most of all I've learned that grief is deep and long, that the first anguish is all-pervading and public – unstoppable – but that as month follows month and no miracle of resurrection occurs, so the calm of control comes with that acceptance while a special and blessed little pocket in the mind keeps all the relevant treasures safe. Thus, strangely composed, I make some additional observations, beliefs, opinions.

Unlike many other mothers of children who have killed themselves, I was mercifully spared the tormented urge to follow, to fight my way into that far land so that I might comfort, take care of, blunt the terrible edge of loneliness. For Baz's going was explained, his purpose clear as glass and his heart's pressure to get to his beloved Suze again past restraint. He would not be lonely, nor would he relish my company as maternal gooseberry. He had broken out of his iron despair, and by his own fighting had escaped his body. The final entry in his diary, a message to the many of us who mourn his going, read: "I am with Suze now, so be *glad* for me". And, in so far as we are able, we keep this light burning.

It is clear to me, looking back, that with Baz's death came a blank disinterest in almost everything else. Life was, overnight, rendered seemingly purposeless. The proper and expected sequence had been ripped into turmoil, placing the child before the parent. The middle-aged woman (myself) mourned the young man where, in the natural way of things, the middle-aged man (Baz) would – 20 or 30 years on – be taking the death of an old lady with gentle relief. I did not experience that common phenomenon of guilt in the sense of "things left undone", but certainly I felt the transposition to be rottenly unfair. And, yes, could some celestial magic have made it possible to bring back Baz and Suze in return for *my* departure, I would not (even now) hesitate to make final plans.

However, through those first long months my leaden will *had* to keep going. Without energy, without any real conviction that I was managing to mask the falling apart of all domestic inclination, I struggled zombie-like through the washing, washing-up, making my awful sunken cakes, seeing the children off to school, stitching on name tapes. The fact that I had continued as a foster mother into my mid-50s, and as such was committed in spite of what might go on externally or within my own soul – all this served, I see now, as a life-saving routine. It got me through.

Even so, layered between my actions, events, conversations and thoughts, lie pictures and scraps and little catches of emotion which *are* Baz. Going into that haze of pre-sleep I actually feel him "visiting" me: sometimes just touching my brow or my shoulder, sometimes scooping me up as though in strong and otherworldly arms: sometimes lying down beside me. His spirit is as real to me as is the inside of my head, and I welcome it with both sadness and joy.

I still do not sleep well: wake at three or four and straight away, before any other slither of thought has a chance, he is there. Usually the film rolls backwards, starting with his terrible despair – the way he walked with his grief, head and shoulders sinking, hands in pockets, without hope; then back perhaps to the time he put his head out of the top deck window of the school bus and only *just* missed catching the lamp-post; or cradling his brown rabbit in Wales; getting drunk at 11 through draining glasses; finding a toy mouse in the gutter at Twickenham and taking it to his heart (Oh, dear gutter mouse, where are you now?); or being born.

And so I tell of my dream, my vision, my glimpse of their ethereal bliss. It happened nine months after his death, and that cycle of gestation is, to me, significant. In this dream I was, as I am now, in my workroom. I was frantically looking for something, rifling papers, up-ending boxes, lifting and putting down – absolutely desperate in my search. It was night, dark; quiet and still but for my rummaging. There was a firm tap, light and repeated just two or three times, at the window. I pulled back the curtain and saw the palm of Baz's hand against the glass pane, flat against the pane like a blessing. Standing outside, his face transfigured by eternal happiness, he was three-dimensional, solid, real. Behind him, greyer, shadier, stood his Suze, and beyond them both the great depth of night. I know with bedrock certainty that these children had come to me for two reasons. First, to show me that all was well, that the time had come for me to begin climbing up from despair. And, second, they had come to say that they were travelling further away; that their bonds with earth were loosening; that the whole universe was to be their home. Yet no word was spoken, nor do I recall their going or my turning from the window. I reconstruct that scene with absolute clarity, carry it in my mind as though painted by Rossetti or Burne Jones. For it was my release, and theirs.

It is fortunate for me that my son was a poet. Through his verses, those which were written over the 73 days between Suze's death and his own, one reads expressions of love and loss so entwined that they are hard to bear without weeping. That he was courting death is set down for all to understand. Mere days after Suze's death, while travelling through the Lake District, he wrote:

> The train moves up the track
> Oblivious to my pain;
> Trying to please me with water,
> Heron, mountain, precious rain.
> Yet, though death is uncertain,
> It rests limpid on my mind
> Now that life's been so dimished by your going.

A fund was set up, the poems were published, the proceeds from sales were used to swell the account of a mammoth appeal for a body scanner for the Brook Hospital in London, the hospital where Suze died. This fund is their memorial and our salve. Working for the fund makes a practicality of grief.

And then there are the roses. One planted for Baz, one for Suze. And the great straggling pussy-willow, in flower against the dark February sky when he took his life away; strewn on his sad box among the daffodils, his yellow teddy and a tiny pair of lambskin slippers he'd worn as a toddler 20 years before. Symbols of both his past and his future.

Our family's past . . . and its future too.